Accessible Storage of Nonbook Materials

Accessible Storage of Nonbook Materials

by Jean Weihs
Illustrated by Cameron Riddle

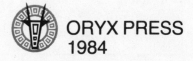
ORYX PRESS
1984

The rare Arabian Oryx is believed to have inspired the myth of the unicorn. This desert antelope became virtually extinct in the early 1960s. At that time several groups of international conservationists arranged to have 9 animals sent to the Phoenix Zoo to be the nucleus of a captive breeding herd. Today the Oryx population is over 400 and herds have been returned to reserves in Israel, Jordan, and Oman.

Copyright © 1984 by The Oryx Press   2|85

Published simultaneously in Canada

Printed and Bound in the United States of America

Library of Congress Cataloging in Publication Data

Weihs, Jean Riddle.
  Accessible storage of nonbook materials.

  Bibliography: p.
  Includes index.
  1. Shelving (for non-book materials).   2. Libraries—
Special collections—Non-book materials.   3. Library
materials—Storage.   4. Libraries—Space utilization.
I. Title.
Z685.W36   1984   025.8'1   84-5281
ISBN 0-89774-084-X

*For Harry
Husband, Father
Friend and Editor*

Table of Contents

Preface

In 1967 I was faced with the task of cataloging the nonbook materials in all the schools in a borough of Metropolitan Toronto. I was undaunted because I believe that, if one can read, one can find the answer to almost any problem. However, it soon became apparent that there was little to read on cataloging nonbook materials. In consulting people who had cataloged their nonbook collections, I found that they were unanimous about one point: the cataloging procedure each had used was not an effective tool for information retrieval. Eventually, we concluded that cataloging rules for nonbook materials should allow all catalog records to be filed in one file and that, unfortunately, no such rules existed at that time.

Nonbook Materials: The Organization of Integrated Collections was written to fill that need. The investigation into the effective cataloging of nonbook materials for an active collection produced some interesting by-products; one of these was the realization that intershelving all or almost all materials in the collection in one classification sequence was a good storage method for circulating libraries. Two school librarians, one elementary and one junior high, allowed us to rearrange their catalogs and collections to test our cataloging theories. We were amazed and delighted to find in both school libraries that the circulation of all materials rose when the collections were intershelved. Therefore, we added a small section on intershelving to our cataloging book.

Since that time I have participated in many workshops, seminars, and lectures on the organization of nonbook materials. Usually, during the question period, someone would raise a question about intershelving. I have also received many letters about storage methods. This book is written in answer to these queries, for those people who now intershelve part or all of their collections and are interested in learning of additional storage devices and for those who want to investigate the intershelving concept.

This is a book of ideas gathered from many sources: from personal experience, from other librarians with multimedia collections, from media specialists, from articles, books, and supply catalogs. It is, in part, an annotated list of containers, devices, and methods for intershelving intended to help libraries decide which ones best fit their resources and objectives.

Introduction

After much research I have concluded that patron-oriented libraries should interfile all catalog records in one all-media catalog. Separate catalogs for each medium result in nonbook materials being used only by patrons who are knowledgeable about the library's catalogs and who are willing and have the time to search through them. In order for entries to be effectively interfiled, the same rules for descriptive cataloging and the same subject heading list should be used for all materials. *The Anglo-American Cataloguing Rules,* second edition (AACR2), is the standard for descriptive cataloging. There are many lists of subject headings, some for use with a general collection, others devised for special collections.

The intershelved collection must be classified by a single classification scheme because items are shelved in one sequence. *Nonbook Materials: The Organization of Integrated Collections,* second edition, by Jean Weihs with Shirley Lewis and Janet Macdonald was written as a companion to AACR2 for libraries that list their collections in one catalog. It also discusses subject analysis for nonbook materials.

Intershelving is recommended for patron-oriented circulating libraries, i.e., school, public, and community college libraries, which do not have an archival function. Such libraries weed their collections of out-of-date or little used items. Their objective is a dynamic collection that can be easily browsed and retrieved by their public.

The terms used for particular nonbook materials in this work are taken from AACR2. The words "library," "librarian," and "library staff" are meant to be synonymous with "resource center," "instructional materials center," "media center," "information center," etc., and their staffs.

This book discusses materials most commonly found in multimedia collections. Librarians who manage other types of media may find useful citations in the bibliography. Illustrations showing methods of intershelving and storage devices do not always depict full shelves and containers because full shelves and containers obliterate the point being illustrated.

The storage of nonbook materials cannot be discussed without some consideration of their care and handling. The recommendations in this book about care and handling are those most feasible for a circulating library where the preservation of materials is not the primary consideration.

Many books and articles are written about media. However, very little is published about what, in my opinion, are the two most important components of a dynamic multimedia library: the staff and the patrons. Without the active involvement of both of these groups, the materials can become unused, expensive junk. Chapters 2 and 3 discuss the importance of staff and patrons and how intershelving can benefit them both.

Apologia for Intershelving Nonprint Materials

A youthful memory calls forth a small town library with books shelved by color and size by a librarian who prided herself on "tidy housekeeping": first, all red books filed shortest to tallest, then green books, blue books. . . . We may smile or shake our heads at this quaint storage method, but the "tidy housekeeper" mentality still has a foothold in the library world. Some librarians insist on the segregation of media because they claim that the shelves do not look attractive (i.e., "messy") when all materials are intershelved. Messiness may be the price to be paid for a dynamic collection. The main purpose of a library is not to present an aesthetic appearance but rather to make available the best and most useful material to the largest number of patrons—and intershelving will accomplish this. There are many, however, who would not agree that intershelving results in unattractive shelves, but they would argue that a variety of media shelved together creates an inviting appearance.

Intershelving is the logical arrangement for a browsing collection. All items on a particular subject are housed together, accessible and retrievable in a single search. This saves time for both patrons and staff because it eliminates the need to search in several places, reduces the number of directional questions a patron may have to ask, and generally eliminates the necessity of retrieving items from a storage area. Intershelving presents the entire range of materials on a given subject in a single location. If nonbook materials are shelved separately, patrons may fail to find useful items.

The discriminatory treatment of nonbook materials may deprive the patron of valuable information and/or enjoyment. If nonbook materials are stored in back rooms, poorly lighted corners, or out-of-the-way places, the patron will either be unaware of their existence or will assume that these materials do not have much value. Intershelving attests to the intellectual significance of all materials.

Intershelving may also introduce a new type of patron to the library— those people who have low reading skills and comprehend more effectively through sight or sound are particularly attracted to nonbook materials. The stigma attached to low reading skills is lessened when patrons use materials from the same shelves. Librarians have found that those who are generally nonreaders—for instance, some students scheduled into the school library—are attracted by items about their favorite hobbies. For example, a motorcycle enthusiast notices a study print on this subject and then examines the other items standing on the shelf—a motion picture loop, a filmstrip, a kit—and eventually reads the books on motorcycles. The desire to read these materials may be an impetus to improve reading skills.

Intershelving has helped teachers develop educational programs. They become more aware of the variety of materials available to meet the diverse needs of students and can direct particular students to nonbook materials.

Many librarians have reported that the introduction of intershelving greatly increased the circulation of *all* materials. In drawing attention to the variety of formats, intershelving leads to information from different perspectives and encourages its exploration. Some librarians were so impressed by the increased use of materials that they took their vertical file material out of filing cabinets and their subject-oriented periodicals off periodical shelves and housed them in pamphlet boxes, Princeton files, or boxes with the rest of the collection on the shelves. Their expectations were fulfilled—the materials were more widely used.

Open Access and Theft

Although, traditionally, machinery has not been considered part of a collection, some libraries have been so committed to optimum public service that they have placed their equipment on open access. Large pieces which will not circulate are bolted down if theft could be a problem. Smaller-sized equipment available for circulation is modified in some libraries to discourage theft. Items marked for circulation may be painted garish, unattractive colors and Sisterson describes "tape recorders screwed down on to large boards (approx. 18 inches square) which are still portable, but not too much so."[1]

The danger of theft and damage, foremost among the reasons cited for segregated storage, brings us to a discussion of the arguments that are raised against intershelving. It is argued that nonbook materials are expensive, easily damaged, and are particularly subject to theft. The 1983 average price of a US hardcover nonfiction book was $30.59.[2] The 1983 prices of many media compare favorably with this; some nonbook materials are expensive, but so are some books. The cost of materials does not appear to have an effect on theft and damage.

Many librarians with intershelved collections have reported that damage and theft have not been major problems. Excerpts from works cited in the bibliography make this point quite clear:

Over a five-year period our book losses averaged slightly under three percent yearly. In comparison, losses of non-book materials showed an average yearly loss as follows: phonodiscs—two percent, slides—two percent, tapes—two percent, transparencies—three percent, film loops—one percent, and filmstrips—one percent. During these five years there were no guards at the doors or any other forms of security.

The problem of easily damaged materials such as record albums can be minimized by either repackaging the resources in sturdier containers or reinforcing the covers of the present containers. . . . In the six years Lord Elgin has been open only one record album has been damaged because of this shelving method. (Stoness, Lord Elgin Secondary School)[4]

7 of the 22 centers conducted . . . research concerning the impact of integrating their media on bookshelves. The research generally consisted of conducting individual background studies prior to the decision to integrate the media. Also, some research was done after the system was in effect for a length of time to determine the extent of vandalism and materials loss. Little difference in the amount of vandalism and materials loss was found with the integrated shelving system. (Hart reporting on a survey of media centres across the United States)[5]

The results of intershelving so far have been that student use of the materials has greatly increased, and their comments have been very favorable. . . . Only a few losses of materials have been sustained, and there has been a minimal amount of materials found in the wrong kits. (Wilson, Windward Community College)[6]

That a majority of the respondents expressed that 'no noticeable difference' had occurred in the amount of theft or damage to nonprint materials is most encouraging. While overall library incidences of theft and damage go unabated, at least the concept of open shelving inherent in multimedia integrated shelving has not demonstrably contributed to the loss or mutilation of nonprint materials at the libraries surveyed. (Donnelly reporting on a survey question answered by 26 southeastern United States academic libraries)[7]

It is clear that patron attitudes toward public property dictate the amount of theft and damage. Both nonbook materials and books will suffer when the library serves patrons who consider theft and vandalism to be acceptable actions. A discussion of societal attitudes toward public property is outside the scope of this book. If such a problem exists in a library, it is possible to achieve some reduction of theft and damage to nonbook materials. Since the majority of nonbook items are nonfiction, placing nonfiction shelves as close as possible to the circulation desk, or any other area where there is supervision, assures constant surveillance. This is particularly effective in a small library. Furthermore, if there is a "run" on a particular medium (the favorite appears to be sound tape cassettes), a dummy or the empty container can be intershelved and the item kept at the circulation desk. The surrogate should have a description of the item or, at the very least, a copy of the catalog record attached to it.

Space for Special Materials

Some critics of intershelving claim that nonbook materials take up too much space on the shelves. Implicit in this remark is the idea that nonbook materials are not as worthwhile as books. If this were the case, it is debatable whether they were worth their purchase price in the first place.

Both books and nonbook materials range in size. Special shelving is made to accommodate oversize books; nonbook materials should be treated in the same manner. Many nonbook materials have containers similar in size to the book collection and are easily intershelved. Media too large for regular shelving should be intershelved in the oversize section.

Storage equipment designed for a particular medium, e.g., a microfilm cabinet, uses valuable space. Some librarians believe that intershelving a collection saves space because more shelving can be built in the places which used to have specialized equipment. Miller notes "when material is stored in pamphlet boxes on book stacks, it consumes less floor space than if it were housed in filing cases." Furthermore, extra space must be allowed in planning library quarters for the opening of file drawers."[8]

Some libraries have small collections of local history and/or items unique to the institution. These may need archival preservation. The bibliography lists some works that deal with the care, handling, and storage of archival materials. If it is possible to duplicate these materials without damaging them, the duplicated copies can be shelved with the regular collection. A description of the more fragile items can also be placed in a pamphlet binder and intershelved. In this way the total collection is readily available to the public.

On the other hand, the amount of time expended on cleaning, cataloging, and/or processing ephemeral materials should not exceed their value to the library. Items of temporary worth can be housed "as is" in a container labelled with a general classification number and shelved at the end of the classification sequence to which they pertain.

In sum, intershelving will make a library truly successful in a way in which success is measured in a library—it will make more materials readily accessible to a larger number of people. But making intershelving work requires the enthusiastic support of staff.

References

1. Joyce Sisterson, Jan Storey, Ian Winkworth, "Letters—Audiovisual Integration," *Audiovisual Librarian,* vol. 7, no. 1 (Winter 1981): 20.

2. Nelson A. Piper, Richard Hume Werking, and Peter Graham, "Library Materials Price Index," *RTSD Newsletter,* vol. 8, no. 2 (May/June 1983): 36.

3. Robert A. Veihman, "Some Thoughts on Intershelving," In *Planning and Operating Media Centers.* Readings from Audiovisual Instruction, 2. (Washington, D.C.: Association for Educational Communications and Technology, 1975): p. 38.

4. B. Jean Stoness, "Integration of Print and Non-print Resources," *Expression,* vol. 1, no. 1 (Spring 1976): 36.

5. Thomas L. Hart, "Dare to Integrate," *Audiovisual Instruction,* vol. 21, no. 8 (October 1976): 18.

6. De Etta Wilson, "On the Way to Intershelving: Elements in the Decision," *Hawaii Library Association Journal,* 33 (1976): 48.

7. Arthur R. Donnelly, "Multimedia Integrated Shelving: A Survey of Its Use in Academic Libraries of the Southeast With Guidelines for Implementation" (Ed Diss., George Peabody College for Teachers, 1978. Ann Arbor, Mich.: University Microfilms, 1979): 51.

8. Shirley Miller, *The Vertical File and Its Satellites: A Handbook of Acquisition, Processing, and Organization.* 2nd ed. Library Science Text Series (Littleton, Colo.: Libraries Unlimited, 1979), p. 48.

Part I
Introducing
Intershelving into the
Library

Chapter 1
The Care and Handling of Staff

A community college hired a new chief librarian to administer a group of libraries in which the previous chief librarian had recently inaugurated intershelving. The new chief librarian was an enthusiastic supporter of the concept, noting that the circulation of all materials had risen and was continuing to rise. She received favorable comments from both academic staff and students concerning the rearranged shelving. However, little by little, almost imperceptively over the next two years, certain types of materials were withdrawn from the shelves and moved to the workroom or other enclosed areas to the point where the collection ceased to be integrated and had to be considered segregated. When asked, the staff gave a variety of reasons why, in their opinion, intershelving was unsatisfactory. A thorough investigation of the reasons for the failure of intershelving revealed that intershelving had been imposed upon the staff without consultation. The staff had resented the arbitrary imposition of intershelving, resulting in the conscious or unconscious determination to prove that this shelving method would not work. Despite the chief librarian's belief that intershelving was a superior system for the library, it was abandoned because of the staff's attitude.

Intershelving works wonderfully with a staff committed to the concept; it will work poorly when the staff is hostile or unenthusiastic. It is important that intershelving be introduced in ways that will gain the staff's cooperation. People tend to be apprehensive of change and many are afraid of appearing awkward and incompetent in using new types of materials and equipment. These fears generate negative attitudes and threaten the success of intershelving.

When nonbook materials are new to a library or have been stored in a separate area, many staff members will know little about them. Before intershelving is inaugurated, it is wise to spend time with the staff on the care and handling of different types of materials, e.g., how to remove a sound disc from a slipcase, how to rewind a filmstrip. This will have three benefits. First, it will make the staff feel more comfortable with the different materials. Second, proper handling will lengthen the life of all materials. Third, patrons are more likely to handle materials properly if staff members do so. It is important that staff members set the example.

In these times of economic restraint most staff members are very busy and have numerous responsibilities. Staff should be made aware that intershelving will release them from the necessity of fetching materials from other areas. Patrons will not ask where to find the nonbook items they want because all items on a subject will be in one area. The staff will have more time to devote to creative work.

An intershelved collection is a patron-oriented collection. Staff members who wish to provide good public service will appreciate intershelving when it is explained. One is led to believe from reading professional literature that all libraries, except those with an archival function, are devoted to the service of their particular publics. However, personal experience and conversations with other librarians and library users support the view that some libraries are operated in a manner most convenient for the staff. These staff members at best give lip service to the patron-oriented concept but resist implementation by voting with their feet. The ways of changing staff attitudes is a broader topic than the scope of this book includes. It is mentioned here by way of noting that management may first have to deal with staff attitudes to public service before intershelving can be discussed.

Each staff member who will be involved with the collection should be given at least one task during the preparation for intershelving. Such tasks could include written instructions on the operation of a piece of equipment or on proper handling techniques for a particular medium. These tasks are described more fully in the next chapter. This early involvement in intershelving can be continued after implementation by assigning to each appropriate staff member in turn an exhibit on a particular topic using all types of media. If only one staff member or a group of staff members is given these tasks, the rest of the staff tends to think that it is none of their affair.

There may be staff members who would be delighted to demonstrate avocational skills. Amateur carpenters can build special shelving; weekend artists can decorate low cost containers. If staff members are too pressed for time to do these things, volunteers might be recruited. Senior citizens who would be bored shelving may be happy to donate their time when it involves skills in which they take pride. Staff or volunteers who contribute directly to a project become interested in making that project a success.

Time spent in preparing the staff for intershelving will be repaid in cooperation, increased public service, and time saved in the future.

Chapter 2
The Care and Handling of Patrons

People need help to become good library patrons. This is especially true when nonbook materials are introduced into the shelving system. As a first step the library should announce its new shelving policy in an interesting and informative manner. An attractive poster placed near the entrance may serve this purpose best. And well labelled shelves are a necessity in a browsing collection.

Many patrons will be unfamiliar with both materials and equipment and can easily and unwittingly cause damage. It is possible to have a staff member explain proper handling techniques when an item is borrowed; however, this is time consuming because it is done on a one-to-one basis and must be repeated with each patron when a nonbook item is borrowed. Also, when the patron uses the item, s/he may not be able to remember the instructions. Often, written instructions seem to be a more efficient and effective method of helping patrons. Instructions should be attached to the item in a prominent place where they are not likely to be overlooked but where they will not interfere with other necessary information, e.g., inside the lid of a container, the verso of a manual's front cover. Instructions will thus be available when needed.

In order to test the comprehensibility of the manufacturers' instructions received with most equipment, they should be given to someone with little or no knowledge of the operation of library equipment. If such a person can interpret these instructions easily, manufacturers' instructions can be duplicated for use with equipment. If s/he experiences any difficulty understanding how to operate equipment, instructions should be rewritten in a "step one, step two" fashion. An instruction sheet must accompany each piece of equipment whether it is operated only in the library or is available for circulation. Because improper use may lead to damage of materials, many libraries offer training sessions for patrons on different pieces of equipment, e.g., 16mm motion picture projectors.

If a library has a severe staff shortage and cannot accommodate even the small amount of time it takes to include an instruction sheet when processing certain items, the next best way to bring this information to the attention of the patron is to have handouts arranged on or near the circulation desk backed by a big poster directing patrons to take one with the material they check out. Many patrons are intimidated by equipment. The sheet of instructions will help, but patrons may need friendly human contact to overcome the fear of looking awkward or incompetent. A word or two indicating that help is available if needed may give confidence.

Proper care and handling techniques can also be advertised on posters placed around the library. Exhibits can be very effective as well. A sound disc left in the sun on the back seat of a car or taken from the bottom of a large pile of discs captures attention when put on display and is likely to be remembered.

Aversions to machinery will be reinforced if equipment is in bad repair or if lighting in the room causes difficulty in reading a screen. Before deciding on the placement of equipment with screens, staff should operate them in different positions at various times of the day so that undesired reflections from light sources can be avoided.

Another help would be to place a box of lintless cloths in the library for the use of patrons who are experiencing difficulties in the correct handling of media. Lintless cloths can be purchased or lintless sewing scraps can be donated by staff and patrons. The poster that directs attention to the box should list what types of cloths are lintless, so that people will be alerted to the proper donations and/or the correct cloths to use at home if an emergency arises.

Furthermore, patrons should be encouraged by both staff and posters to use pencils rather than pens when taking notes. Pens may leak and may cause marks that are more difficult to remove than pencil marks. While some types of materials are not as sensitive to pressure as others, patrons should be actively discouraged from writing on paper placed on top of library materials.

Assessing Damages

All materials deteriorate eventually. Handling of any sort contributes to this deterioration; rough handling speeds it. A library should establish criteria as to what constitutes normal wear and tear and apply these criteria consistently when assessing damage to materials. It is not reasonable to accept without penalty a book returned with a loose signature while charging for a scratched sound disc. Money will have to be spent repairing or replacing the book. A rebound book with its narrowed inner margin is less satisfying to use, as is the scratched disc. An inconsistent policy will discourage the use of materials for which there is a heavier damage penalty.

If a penalty is to be assessed, there needs to be an established method of indicating both existing damage before the item is loaned and any additional damage on return. Hostile reactions to damage charges may be minimized if the policy on punitive damage and the method of determining the charge is displayed prominently.

Patrons will report damage or loss if the consequences of doing so do not result in unreasonable fines. A statement encouraging the reporting of damage or loss should be added to instruction sheets, posters, exhibits, etc. Patron cooperation can save staff time. In addition, time can also be saved and frustration avoided if missing parts are noted on the container or in another prominent place. When the missing parts seriously affect the utility of an item, it should be withdrawn from circulation.

Most people do not want to be destructive. Ignorance and carelessness may be at the root of the problems. Indeed, many people display cooperation and constructive attitudes toward matters involving the betterment of community life. For example, they will travel a considerable distance out of their way to take empty containers to a glass recycling depot. A knowledgeable, tactful, and alert library staff can develop this public goodwill and help people to be good patrons.

Chapter 3
The Care and Handling of Nonbook Materials

The optimum conditions for the care, handling, and storage of materials preclude their use. Perfect storage is incompatible with the function of a circulating collection. Therefore, the preservation of materials should be balanced against public convenience. Materials must be handled during receiving, cataloging, processing, shelving, and circulation. Comments on care and handling are intended to suggest the least detrimental ways of caring for and handling nonbook materials in intershelved collections.

Conservation procedures undertaken when an item is processed for the shelves are a wise investment because these procedures are much simpler and less expensive in time and materials than those involved in damage repair. The amount of conservation devoted to a particular item should be weighed against the replacement cost and the ephemeral nature of the subject content. For example, little effort should be devoted to the preservation of some road maps, first, because they cost little or nothing and, second, because they may be superceded next year.

Building, Design, and Environmental Considerations

The building or area within a building that houses a library can be a positive or negative force for the conservation of its contents. Attics and basements should be avoided because heavy rain and melting snow may cause leaks, and floods can be disastrous. Fluctuations in temperature and relative humidity are one of the more detrimental factors. Temperature changes cause contractions and expansions which will hasten the deterioration of many materials. Many items are made from several component materials that absorb and lose heat and expand and contract at different rates leading to structural breakdown. Direct sunlight, lighting fixtures, heating units such as radiators and vents, and uninsulated outer walls can cause temperature fluctuations in nearby items. Also, items absorb and lose moisture at different rates. High humidity promotes mold, mildew, fungi, and oxidation; low humidity causes brittleness and static electricity which attracts dust.

Good care and handling procedures dictate that the library be air conditioned and a constant temperature and relative humidity be maintained. The decision to lower temperatures and/or shut down air conditioning systems overnight or on weekends should be examined carefully in light of daily climatic conditions. A reasonable compromise must be struck between patron and staff comfort and the need to preserve materials when deciding what temperature and relative humidity (RH) to maintain. Ellison reports that Library of Congress researchers list 69°F plus or minus 1°F and 49% RH plus or minus 3% RH as the proper atmosphere for a multimedia library. The National Library of Canada recommends 19°–20°C and 50% RH plus or minus 5%.[1] Thompson, whose booklet has been edited by the IFLA Round Table on Audiovisual Media, states that 81°C plus or minus 3°C and 50% RH plus or minus 10% is acceptable to all library material.[2]

Lighting is another problem. Readers need light. Bright, sunny libraries have a welcoming look, and libraries have worked long and hard to rid themselves of the "dark, dusty" reputation. But light, especially sunlight, is damaging to nearly all library materials. Everyone knows what happens to papers left on a windowsill or to curtains covering a south window. Therefore, windows should be protected by blinds or curtains or have window panes specially treated to filter ultraviolet rays, for it is the ultraviolet rays that do the damage. Ultraviolet rays from fluorescent lighting can be reduced, but not eliminated, by fitting the tubes with special covers or by purchasing special coated tubes. Incandescent lighting does not emit high levels of ultraviolet rays. However, it produces more heat and uses more energy than fluorescent lighting. A choice of the lighting system to be used should be made after an examination of all design criteria.

Dirt and pollution of all kinds also cause deterioration. Since it is impossible to maintain a sterile environment in a patron-oriented library, libraries can only try to ameliorate the dirt/pollution problem. Industrial pollution, exhaust fumes, the salt in the sea air, and many other components of the air we breathe can affect library materials adversely. Some buildings are designed with positive pressure which helps to keep dust out. Good building construction or repair also prevents the infestation of insects and rodents.

An air conditioning system which includes filtration can reduce these air contaminants to insignificant levels. Window units do not provide the protection achieved by central air conditioning systems. If air conditioning is an impossible dream, humidifiers and/or dehumidifiers should be installed. It is important that temperature and relative humidity be measured and recorded to provide indication and warning when corrective action is required.

There are other hazards to be avoided as well. Cleaning materials should not be housed near the collection. Paint, cleaning solvents, turpentine, and similar materials give off fumes which may have an adverse effect on some materials. Plants should not be placed where water spills will damage the collection. Rubber bands, paper clips, and adhesive tapes should be avoided because they contain acids which can cause deterioration or stains which are almost impossible to remove.

Cleanliness

Libraries should attempt to have as clean an environment as is possible without discouraging the use of materials by unreasonable rules. For example, although it is desirable, few patrons will wash their hands before touching materials. However, patrons can be shown the way to handle the particular materials that will be damaged by fingermarks and skin oils. In addition, smoking, eating, and drinking in the library should be prohibited. The particles from smoke settle on materials and the crumbs and drops from food and drink attract insects which feed on the chemicals in paper and other materials.

All media should be clean before being added to the collection. In particular, donations should be carefully inspected for mold or insect infestation.

Workroom Supplies and Procedures

A well equipped workroom will facilitate the proper care and handling of nonbook materials. A supply of lintless gloves or cloths, distilled water, and acid-free containers should be included in the supplies maintained in the workroom. The gloves/cloths will be readily available when materials are handled; the distilled water can be used for the inexpensive routine maintenance of some materials; and the presence of acid-free containers which are necessary housing for some media will ensure that unsuitable containers are not used "in the meantime." All of these are inexpensive or possibly free if the staff cooperates in bringing lintless scraps from home and saving containers previously used for film materials. The workroom should also contain a high powered flexible lamp to enable an appraisal of disc surfaces, filmstrip scratches, etc., if the library has a policy of damage assessment.

Clean equipment will help keep software clean; it is usually easier to clean the hardware than the software. When equipment is not in use, compartments should be closed and dust covers replaced. (Some librarians, however, do not cover equipment while the library is open because they believe covers discourage use.) Operating manuals usually suggest suitable cleaning fluids and outline a program of regular maintenance which will extend the life of the equipment. Systematic hardware maintenance is more likely if the operating manuals can be retrieved easily and staff members are conditioned to return them to the proper file after use.

Preventing Damage and Loss

Software should not be forced on or off the hardware. If this cannot be done with relative ease, the equipment should be serviced. It may be cheaper to replace old equipment in poor condition than to purchase new software because of the damage caused by faulty hardware.

It is important to note that temperature differences between hardware and software will affect playback and may cause damage to the software. Media and equipment should be allowed to return to room temperature naturally before play; neither heating nor cooling should be hastened.

A circulating library must expect some mishaps when materials leave the building. The most a library can do is to provide protective circulation containers and instructions on proper handling and care procedures. Most materials will be returned in good condition and it is not economically feasible or politically desirable to examine all nonbook items for damage or loss after every loan. Books are not examined on return.

The labels on media designed for insertion into equipment must be firmly affixed because loose labels can cause havoc first to the machine and subsequently to the software. Also, adequate labelling will help to decrease the loss of parts. Labelling should indicate ownership and the item to which the component belongs. It may not be possible or practical to label every part in every set. A decision about the amount of labelling will revolve around its cost effectiveness and the importance of the components to the utilization of the whole.

Many-part items can be weighed out and in on scales that are able to detect a difference of as little as one gram. The cost of such an expensive scale can be justified only if the collection includes numerous items made up of many expensive or difficult-to-replace components.

In developing a policy statement on examination procedures and punitive charges for damage and loss, the basic consideration is cost. The very expensive media, such as 16mm motion pictures, should be examined for damage. On the other hand, it is not cost effective for staff to check each part of a many-piece set when the replacement value of the set is less than the salary cost involved. Media should also be examined in instances where unrepaired minor damage will lead to serious destruction, e.g., torn sprocket holes may cause a 16mm motion picture projector to chew up many feet of film.

Good care and handling will lengthen the life of a collection. A circulating library must provide information and entertainment while maintaining materials in a useful state. This is a delicate balancing act. The suggestions in later chapters for ways of caring for and handling specific media are made with this thought in mind.

References

1. Joyce M. Banks, *Guidelines for Prevention Conservation* (Ottawa, ON: Committee on Conservation/Preservation of Library Materials, 1981), p. 4.

2. Anthony Hugh Thompson, *Storage, Handling and Preservation of Audiovisual Materials*. AV in Action, 3. (The Hague: Nederlands Bibliotheek en Lektuur Centrum, 1983), p. 8.

Chapter 4
General Storage Considerations

Total intershelving is the ideal arrangement for a browsing collection and should be effected wherever possible. This means that every item in the collection is housed in one classification sequence. (See Figure 1.) However, there may be reasons why this cannot be accomplished. For example, shelving space may be too limited to provide the 12½ inch high space necessary for housing sound discs; an area may be subject to vibrations which affect videotapes; theft of sound cassettes may be a problem. A good solution to such problems is to have well-labelled dummies act as surrogates in these areas. This allows some browsing and maintains the sequence. It is especially helpful if the labelling on surrogates includes clear instructions where the item can be obtained.

Figure 1. Total intershelving.

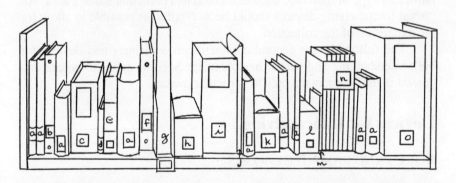

a. book; b. binder containing microfiches; c. box containing filmstrips; d. book-like album containing a single sound cassette; e. videotape cassette in container; f. binder containing slides; g. clip-on holder containing a motion picture in a box; h. motion picture loop cartridge in container; i. box containing slide carousel; j. envelope containing a single Viewmaster slide; k. microfilm reel in container; l. box containing microopaque cards; m. pamphlet binder containing a single picture; n. Princeton file holding issues of a current periodical; o. kit housed in a box

Partial intershelving is a second solution in which all items are on open access, but they are not in one sequence. There are three types of partial intershelving:

1. Media in the same classification range are stored on one shelf. The items in boxes and other book-like containers are intershelved with books on one part of the shelf. Other media are housed in some type of storage device on another part of the shelf. This is the best method of partial intershelving because items with similar subject content are in close proximity.
2. Some media, housed in boxes and other suitable containers, are intershelved. Other media are stored on separate shelves, generally called media shelves, at the end of the appropriate classification sequence. This is satisfactory only in sections of the collection where the beginning of the classification sequence on the regular shelves is not widely separated from the beginning of the same sequence on the media shelves. Materials are likely to be overlooked if many shelves separate the two.
3. Far less satisfactory are freestanding storage units because these separate materials in a substantial way. These units are justified only when shelf space is limited and open floor storage is the only room left for collection expansion.

Dummies and one or all of these methods of partial intershelving can be used in a library for a variety of needs. One method may be applied to a particular type of material, another method to a particular storage area. All partial intershelving devices should be as flexible as possible to allow for the expansion of the collection.

The following are general comments on containers and devices for both intershelving and partial intershelving. Specific applications are discussed in the chapters devoted to particular media.

Devices for Intershelving

BOXES AND PAMPHLET BOXES

Some manufacturers market their products in sturdy boxes that are designed for shelving and are adequately labelled. After processing, these boxes can be intershelved.

Unfortunately, some materials are packaged in containers that are not likely to endure reasonable handling, while some have no containers at all. The library worker is then faced with decisions.

If an item is in an attractive but inadequate box which is descriptive of its contents, an effort should be made to prepare it for shelving. Some manufacturers, in order to pare costs, do not reinforce corners. Reinforced corners may be all a box needs to make it durable. Boxes can also be strengthened with a covering of adhesive transparent sheeting. This may be expensive, but it might be worth the cost to preserve a truly useful box.

Some manufacturers package materials in boxes that are larger than needed for the contents and which, if shelved, would take up unnecessary space. These materials should be repackaged.

Boxes provide an easy, though not the only, means of intershelving. They sit on shelves very much like books and provide protection for their contents. There are many different types of boxes available both commercially and casually; the decision of what type of boxes to use for a particular medium depends on the nature of the material, the degree of preservation required, and the library's goals and objectives.

Materials that react to the chemicals in ordinary paper products, such as film, must be housed in acid-free boxes. An archival pen will provide a quick reading on acidity levels if there is some doubt whether a container is acid-free. Items that are difficult to replace and will have a long term use should be stored in boxes of archival quality. There are many types of archival boxes available commercially, but they are expensive.

There are also many types of nonarchival boxes for sale—cardboard, fiberboard, corrugated, plasticized, etc. Some have inserts that hold the contents in place. These can be found in any library supply company's catalog. Some of these boxes can be purchased flat at a lower cost and hand assembled in the library.

A library may wish to have the actual item on the shelf seen by the patron without the barrier of a closed opaque box. This can be achieved by the use of transparent plastic boxes, both transparent and opaque pamphlet boxes, and Princeton files. Princeton files are only useful for items that are large enough to be held securely in the file. Pamphlet boxes are available in several styles, e.g., cut corner, open back, cardboard, plastic, corrugated. The cheapest ones are purchased flat and assembled by the library staff.

It is easy for library staff to obtain commercially made boxes because most library supply companies display a variety of boxes in their catalogs. Therefore, the following discussion will concentrate on economical boxes not marketed in these catalogs.

Inexpensive box cutouts can be purchased flat from a local box manufacturer and easily assembled by the library staff. This very low cost packaging can be even cheaper if ordered by a group of libraries because a larger run will result in lower unit costs.

Some boxes may be acquired casually—library supply boxes, gift boxes, etc. Staff members can be alerted to preserve sturdy boxes for use in storage. Local druggists or camera stores may be willing to donate used boxes, many of which will be acid-free.

Unfortunately, the great majority of low-cost boxes are unattractive and some casually acquired boxes, such as shoe boxes, may have unwanted information written on them. This information can be covered with leftover paint or wallpaper. An attractive brochure should be kept until the item is received and then used to decorate a noninformative container.

It takes time to make cheap boxes attractive, but this may have benefits for the library. In addition to obtaining attractive boxes, a school library can advertise its nonbook collection by cooperating with an art teacher and a public library can gain publicity by holding a contest for the creation of appropriate box decoration. The activity associated with box decoration also offers an opportunity to reach out to a new group of people. There are individuals who would not volunteer to shelve but would be happy to use their artistic talents. For instance, someone who enjoys wrapping presents may find decorating media boxes a challenge.

Even if staff members or volunteers are not available for box decoration, a brief description of the contents and equipment needed for utilization should be prominently displayed on the front of the box to increase the ease of browsing and reduce the amount of handling. In a library with a card catalog, an extra annotated catalog card could be used for this purpose.

BOOK-LIKE ALBUMS

These containers have been designed in response to an expressed interest in intershelving. The albums generally have vinyl covers and rigid plastic interiors molded to hold specific numbers and types of media. The "snap-in" compartments maintain a firm hold on sound cassettes, filmstrip canisters, and slide carousels. Some have permanently affixed small boxes in which slides can be stored. Many have clear plastic pockets for manuals, charts, and other two-dimensional materials. In some albums a spine window allows the patron to read the title on the filmstrip canister lid or on the cassette container. There is a wide range of albums adapted for various combinations of media.

There are three features which detract from these otherwise useful albums. The first is price. They are more expensive than many of the other storage methods described in this book. Second, they are less flexible. They are designed for a specific medium or combination of media; other storage methods, e.g., boxes, binders, hang-ups, can be used by a variety of media. If a filmstrip housed in a hanging bag is discarded, the bag can be used to store another medium. Third, many albums are designed to house slide carousels or sound and micrcomputer cassettes without their boxes. Dirt can affect the quality of tape playback and damage slides. These media should be protected by closed containers during storage. Albums that lock with a dust tight closure are preferred for media that will be stored unboxed.

There are other book-like albums made of paper products designed to hold one or two microcomputer cassettes and sound cassettes and cartridges. These are better storage units because they accommodate containers and are cheaper to purchase.

BINDERS

Intershelving can be accomplished very effectively by housing media in suitable binders made of materials rigid enough to be self-supporting. Ring binders are particularly versatile because plastic pages designed to hold various sizes and shapes can be purchased or library-made. These transparent pages allow the items to be browsed easily yet keep them protected from direct contact with fingers. The whole binder can be circulated, or individual pages can be removed for circulation. Ring binders receive rough handling from students in their school work and will most certainly stand up to the gentler demands of normal library use.

A library may wish to shelve a single item but may not want to use the space or afford the cost of a ring binder. In this case the item can be housed in a pressboard pamphlet binder by attaching:

1. One-sheet items to any convenient place inside the binder.
2. Items with a single fold to the spine of the binder.
3. Items with more than one fold to an inside edge.

A set that is too large for a ring binder can be placed in an open back pamphlet tie binder or a hinge binder.

CLIP-ON HOLDERS

Clip-on holders can be purchased in several sizes suitable for a variety of materials. Because they are self-supporting, they can be placed anywhere on the shelves. They are excellent units for intershelving in those libraries which want to shelve their collections with as little repackaging as possible.

Almost-shelf-tall, narrow units give support to items that cannot stand vertically by themselves such as pictures, maps, transparencies, sound discs, videodiscs, and microcomputer disks. Filmstrips are held firmly in slanted clip-ons which may have a compartment for manuals. Small items such as sound tapes, microfilms, and motion picture loops, which could be pushed inadvertently out of sight to the back of the shelf, are kept in their proper place by shallow clip-ons. There are clip-ons designed for small multimedia kits.

The holders are attached to the shelves by built-in bracket clips. When holders house one item, one set, or items with the same classification number, the call number or classification can be affixed to the clip on the lower front edge of the shelf. This aids quick shelving and the identification of items with spines too narrow to permit their labels to be seen immediately.

Their steel construction is not only self-supporting but also supports adjacent materials, and some libraries use these units as bookends. In this position the holders become devices for partial intershelving. The same steel construction also makes them almost impervious to destruction from normal library handling. However, they cannot accommodate the range of media or number of items which are possible with other types of devices.

The holders are designed either for wood or for steel shelves. Both styles are surprisingly inexpensive; those designed for steel shelves are two-thirds the cost of those for wood shelves. The price is competitive with corrugated fiberboard containers and cheaper than corrugated plastic containers and vinyl book-like containers.

MODULAR UNITS

A modular unit is another device that will hold small items at the front of the shelf. Cube or similarly shaped units specially designed to hold sound and microcomputer cassettes or 16mm microfilm reels and 8-track tape cartridges or 35mm microfilm reels can be shelved singly or can be attached together both horizontally and vertically to house a many-piece set. They are sturdy enough to withstand normal library usage and are reasonably priced. One side of the unit is open so that labels can be seen. The units are spacious enough to accommodate a container which gives added protection to the item being stored.

Other units, sometimes called "mini-cabinets," have similar characteristics but do not lock together. Each unit holds more than twice the number of items and is approximately the same per unit cost as interlocking modules. Double size "mini-cabinets" are available; however, capacity can be increased by placing single units side by side.

Interlocking units are better suited to intershelving because they are more flexible. Both types of modules can be used for partial intershelving by placing a single unit or several units on one end of a shelf.

Devices for Partial Intershelving

HANGING DEVICES

The most popular hanging storage devices appear to be hanging bags because they are inexpensive and versatile. The bags are available in seven sizes to accommodate items with a variety of shapes. Their clear polyethylene construction allows the patron to see the contents, thereby reducing the handling of individual items. But the bags do impose some limitations in size and weight of contents. The largest bag is 14×21 inches and its construction cannot support the weight of heavy items.

There are three storage methods for hanging bags:

1. Part shelf storage. Free standing racks, which are available in four sizes, are placed at one end of a shelf in the appropriate classification sequence. This method of hanging bag storage is preferred because it keeps the contents of the bags closer to similarly classified materials than the other two methods.

    When there is only one bag to be housed on a particular shelf, libraries that have wire bookends suspended from the underside of the shelf above can use these as the hanging device.

2. Separate shelf for hanging bag device. This is a variation of the media shelf discussed later in this chapter, in which a whole shelf is devoted to the storage of nonbook materials. It is situated at the end of the shelves holding books and, possibly, book-like containers with the same classification. This method has three advantages over media shelves; it can hold a larger range of sizes; manuals can be stored with the items; and intershelving items within the device is not hampered by partitions.

    If a library has closed end shelving, the bags can be hung on an adjustable tension rod held by free standing supports. If a library has open end shelving, the bags can be hung on a rod supported at each end by brackets attached to the standards for the rest of the shelving.

3. Storage outside the shelves. A library that has limited shelf space may store hanging bags outside the regular shelving. A bar can be mounted on a section of the wall not used for shelving or even on a suitable door. If the available wall space is very small, the bags can be hung on utility brackets attached to the wall near the appropriate classification. This is an excellent way of using odd bits of space in cramped quarters. Bags can also be hung from pegboard brackets. Pegboard can be cut to fit any space.

    Revolving floor stands for storing bags can be used if no wall space is available. These should be placed as close to the appropriate classification as possible. These stands are much more expensive and less effective than the other storage devices for hanging bags.

There are other more sophisticated hanging device systems designed to house specific formats such as maps, technical drawings, or sound discs. Some of these can be adapted to partial intershelving. They are much more expensive than hanging bags.

Large items can be hung on dress racks or other types of hanging devices not normally found in libraries. Sometimes these racks can be purchased cheaply at distress sales.

MEDIA SHELF

Some libraries prefer to house nonbook materials on a separate shelf. For example, there may be several shelves of books in the Dewey classification sequence 520–529 followed by a shelf of small- to medium-sized nonbook materials and a shelf of large items each arranged in the 520–529 sequence. The latter, which is not termed a ''media shelf,'' is frequently a bottom or top shelf and does not have any special fittings to assist in housing media. A media shelf is designed specifically to house nonbook materials and is usually tilted at a 45° angle to facilitate browsing.

Many commercially produced media shelves have devices which hold specific types of media in rigid or semi-rigid positions. One of the most flexible and inexpensive media shelves is pictured in Figure 13, which is discussed in Chapter 6. This shelf is fitted with bars that can be adjusted when the collection is shifted.

Unfortunately, media shelves do not accommodate manuals.

CARTMOBILES

Cartmobiles are book trucks adapted for media storage. They are generally used to solve two problems: first, if a library's shelf space cannot accommodate an increase in the collection, book trucks with fittings to house nonbook materials can increase storage space. Second, materials which are too large to fit on shelves can be housed on book trucks which have flat shelves.

In both cases the book truck should be positioned as close as possible to the shelves containing materials with the same subject content.

Part II
Storage of Various Media for Greater Access

Chapter 5
Sound Discs

Because the 12 inch, 33⅓ rpm long-playing vinyl sound disc format is the one most frequently found in circulating libraries, this chapter will deal principally with it. Much of this content can also be applied to the seven-inch diameter, 45 rpm discs found in some collections.

The size and fragility of sound discs discourages many libraries from incorporating them into their intershelved collections. Some libraries do not have sufficient shelf space to allow 12½ inch high shelves in sections where only a few discs would be stored. In these instances, open access storage close to the appropriate classification section may be advisable. The same approach may be taken when libraries possess only music sound discs, all of which would be shelved in a small range of classification numbers.

Different methods of storage ranging from total intershelving to "non-shelf" open access devices may be used for various sections of the collection depending on the numbers of sound discs to be housed. For example, libraries that have nonmusic as well as music sound discs may intershelve the former, while placing the latter in "nonshelf" open access devices.

Another factor to be taken into consideration when making storage decisions is the heavy weight of sound discs. If a library does not have heavy duty shelving, it must limit the number of discs to be placed on any one shelf.

Care and Handling

Warping. If a disc slipcase is received in a cellophane wrapper, the wrapper should be removed immediately. It is highly sensitive to temperature change and may shrink causing the disc to warp. Warping can also be caused by housing discs near sources of heat or by improper storage methods. An amateur sound disc buff suggests the following method for restoring warped discs to their original shape. Place the disc in a lukewarm oven between two pieces of plate glass each ¼ inch thick and larger than the disc. Turn the oven off and allow the disc and pieces of glass to cool down in the oven undisturbed until the oven and its contents reach room temperature. I cannot verify this method of "de-warping" in any printed source. However, I did try it on one disc with satisfactory results.

Protective covering. Attractive and/or informative slipcases should be protected by transparent durable covers because most slipcases will not stand up to constant handling. Inexpensive covers are available commercially.

Discs should be stored within slipcases in polyethylene liners. Many producers package discs in liners suitable for storage. However, paper or glassine inner liners should be discarded unless they are acid-free. Watch especially for poor quality paper which can shed paper dust. The cost of replacing liners is low.

Cleanliness. A clean disc has a longer life and greater fidelity. Staff should resist the temptation to blow on discs to remove dust because particles contained in breath moisture may be deposited. Many aids for cleaning discs are available commercially including equipment attachments, mechanical devices, and chemical solutions.

There is a controversy among experts over the efficacy and safety of washing sound discs in distilled water and liquid detergent. The discs in a circulating collection will need regular cleaning because they may be handled by careless users on improperly maintained equipment. Library staff members should experiment by washing discs in a certain section of the collection and judging the results before investing in more expensive methods. Several books in the bibliography give instructions on washing techniques. Unfortunately, the authors differ somewhat on the proper method.

The risk of dust contamination will be reduced if the opening of the polyethylene liner is at a 90° angle to the opening of the slipcase. This has the additional benefit of holding the disc more securely in the slipcase.

The disc surface and the stylus should not be touched because the body oils deposited will attract dust and provide areas hospitable to the growth of mold. Only the rim and the label should be touched when handling the disc. Figure 2 shows the placement of thumb and fingers when handling a disc. If

Figure 2. Hands should not touch the surface of the disc.

the slipcase is too narrow to allow the entrance of a hand, the disc should be removed with the aid of a clean piece of lintless cloth or gloves. A lintless cloth should also be used to remove any fingermarks found on improperly handled discs.

The turntable mat should be covered with a thin polyethylene disc which can be purchased or cut from a spare polyethylene liner. This will help to keep the discs clean because the mat cover can be wiped with a barely damp lintless cloth before use, thus removing any dust which might be on the turntable.

The polyethylene mat cover has a second function; it indicates the presence of static build-up, which attracts dust. If the sound disc is carrying a static charge, the polyethylene mat cover will stick to its underside. The degree to which the polyethylene clings to the sound disc gives some indication of the strength of the charge. Anti-static agents should be used to eliminate static build-up; works in the bibliography discuss various ways of accomplishing this. An easy temporary method of discharging static is to wipe the sound disc with a barely damp, soft, lintless cloth.

Storage

The ideal way to preserve discs in storage is to lay each disc singly on a flat surface which provides equal support at all points. This is obviously impractical for a library because of the amount of space required. Discs cannot be piled horizontally one on top of the other because the pressure on the discs in the lower part of the pile causes warping and surface imprinting. Therefore, library collections should be shelved vertically. It is best to have the discs in a fully vertical position because off-vertical stacking can cause warp. When patrons borrow discs, enough space may be created in the shelving to allow discs to tilt. This can be corrected by having temporary blocks available which can be placed in the space until the discs are returned. On the other hand, discs should not be stored so tightly that shelving and retrieval causes grinding.

In busy circulating collections off-vertical stacking, e.g., browser bins, may not be a problem because the discs may not sit in one spot long enough to warp and public convenience may be a higher priority than disc durability. Off-vertical stacking should be avoided in those sections of the collection that circulate infrequently.

Bins must be designed so that discs will not be able to slip under other discs, thus causing damage. The bin should have a nonskid bottom and its construction should not allow discs to lean too far backward or forward.

Intershelving of Sound Discs

BOXES (Figure 16a)

Most commercially produced albums in boxed sets can be inter-shelved. Sturdy boxes specifically designed to house sound discs are available commercially for those items received without boxes or in inadequate boxes. If needed, inserts can be placed in the boxes to hold the discs in a vertical position. Boxes shelved in situations where they might fall over can be placed in clip-on holders discussed below.

CLIP-ON HOLDERS (Figure 28g)

Tall, narrow clip-on holders are self-supporting and will allow sound discs to be housed in a vertical position in the proper classification sequence on the shelf. Their width, generally slightly under two inches, provides assurance that, after some discs have been removed for circulation, the remaining discs will tilt only slightly. The information on the spine of the slipcase can be seen and the disc is readily available for circulation.

A general description of clip-on holders can be found earlier in this chapter.

VERTICAL STACKING IN FREESTANDING CONTAINERS
(Figure 22d)

This method of storing sound discs was developed by the Library of Congress as part of a research study on archival collections. [1]   The Library of Congress recommends that twenty 12 inch discs be housed in a cardboard container. One end of the container is open to display the information on the spine of the slipcase and to allow easy access to the discs.

This convenient and economical storage system is well suited to circulating multimedia collections. The containers can be shelved in the appropriate place in the classification system and the size of the containers adapted to varying storage needs. Care must be taken to ensure that the cardboard in the containers is strong enough to maintain the discs in a fully vertical position. If a container houses only one or two discs, either permanently or temporarily, blocks can be placed in the spaces to keep the disc(s) vertical. A local box manufacturer may be able to supply this type of container in appropriate sizes quite inexpensively.

Freestanding units made of transparent rigid plastic are also available commercially. These have an interlocking device if greater capacity is needed. They are more expensive and have less potential for flexibility than cardboard containers.

Partial Intershelving of Sound Discs

MULTIMEDIA SHELF WITH MOVABLE SPACING PANELS (Figure 3e)

Vertical stacking in compartments separated by fixed spacing panels three and one-half to four inches apart is recommended for archival storage. This can be adapted to circulating collections by having the end of a regular shelf fitted with movable spacing panels. If the library staff includes a good carpenter, the cost of such shelving adaptations would be low.

Figure 3. Multimedia shelf with movable spacing panels.

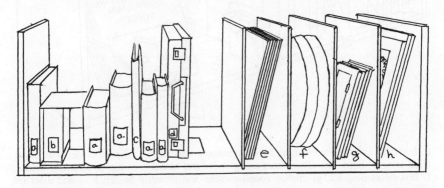

a. book; b. microfilm or motion picture loop cartridge in a stacking module; c. pamphlet binder containing two dimensional material in a binder page; d. slide file; e. sound discs; f. motion pictures in film cans; g. transparencies; h. pictures

MULTIMEDIA SHELF WITH PULL OUT RACKS OR BINS (Figure 4h)

Sound discs may be housed in bins or racks on sliding tracks which are attached to one end of a shelf. The bin or rack is pulled out for easy access; when not in use, the unit is pushed back so that its front is flush, or almost flush, with the rest of the shelf. The decision to use bins or racks is based on whether public convenience or disc durability is given priority; bins allow better accessibility, racks hold discs in a more vertical position.

MULTIMEDIA SHELF WITH COMMERCIAL RACK (Figure 5g)

This is probably the easiest and cheapest method of partial intershelving for sound discs. Racks are available at a low price in most stores that sell sound discs. A rack placed on one end of a shelf holds discs with their spines facing the public. Many racks can be purchased in, or cut to, appropriate sizes. The racks can be readily moved unless the library has had the racks attached to the shelves for greater stability.

Figure 4. Multimedia shelf with pull out rack.

a. book; b. envelope containing two-dimensional materials; c. clip-on holder with small slide box; d. book-like album containing slides and manual; e. clip-on filmstrip holder; f. box containing kit; g. clip-on sound cassette and filmstrip holder; h. sound discs on pull-out rack

Figure 5. Multimedia shelf with rack.

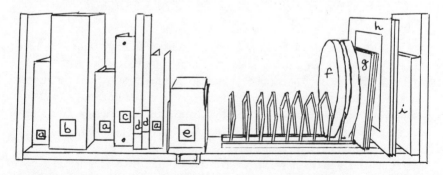

a. book; b. diorama in box; c. binder containing microcomputer cassettes; d. pamphlet binder containing folded two-dimensional material; e. motion picture loop cartridge and container in clip-on holder; f. motion picture reel in container; g. sound disc in slipcase; h. pictures; i. game in box

HANGING DEVICES (Figure 6)

Some of the hanging bags discussed in Chapter 4 are large enough to accommodate 12 inch or smaller discs. The bags do not provide support or protection for easily damaged items; discs should be stored by this method only when they are not crowded and subject to pressure. Albums and well packaged single discs are better suited to this type of storage.

Figure 6. Hanging bags.

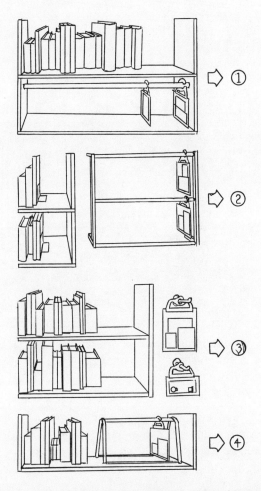

1. full shelf storage; 2. bars for hanging bags mounted on wall beside appropriate classification; 3. utility brackets for hanging bags mounted on wall beside appropriate classification; 4. free-standing racks for hanging bags placed on shelf at end of appropriate classification sequence

CARTMOBILES (Figure 7)

Figure 7. Cartmobile with racks.

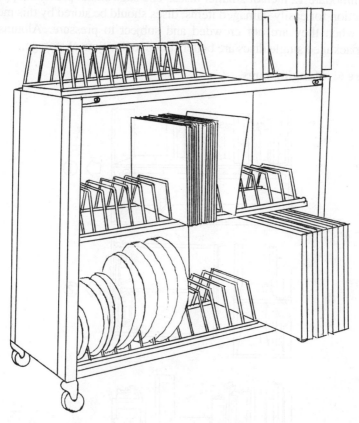

Cartmobiles containing racks for sound discs are used where shelf space is limited. A general description of cartmobiles is found in Chapter 4.

MOBILE RECORD BINS

Where the classification has many sound discs, e.g., 780s, and little shelf space, properly constructed mobile bins may house sound discs. These bins should be placed near the appropriate shelves.

Reference

1. A. G. Pickett and M. M. Lemcoe, *Preservation and Storage of Sound Recordings* (Washington, DC: Library of Congress, 1959), pp. 41–42.

Chapter 6
Magnetic Tapes (Computer Tapes, Sound Tapes, Videotapes)

Multimedia collections in circulating libraries frequently contain reel-to-reel sound tapes, sound cassettes, and videocassettes; some libraries also possess sound cartridges, reel-to-reel videotapes, and microcomputer cassette tapes. Computer tapes that are part of research and specialized collections are not usually found in circulating libraries. Although this chapter does not deal with these computer tapes, some of the general comments may apply to them also.

Tapes housed in cartridges or cassettes are better protected against careless or inexpert handling than reel-to-reel tapes. Unfortunately, sound cartridges and cassettes may not have the fidelity of reel-to-reel sound tapes. The library will have to balance the sophistication of the patrons' needs against the convenience of the cassette or cartridge format.

Care and Handling

Cleanliness. It is essential to keep magnetic tape as dust-free as possible because dust can cause dropouts and sound distortion. Tapes should be kept in containers when not in use, and those not in cassettes or cartridges should be placed in polyethylene bags sealed with tape or with the edges of the bag folded over. Playback equipment should be clean and heads demagnetized periodically to prevent build-up of static electricity which attracts dust. Dust must be removed from all parts of an empty reel before use.

As with discs, tape should never be touched because oil from fingermarks deposited on the tape holds dust. If tape must be handled (for example in splicing), lintless gloves must be worn. A long leader tape at the beginning and end of the magnetic tape will ensure that only the leader is handled during threading. In addition, leader tape will reduce the stress on the main tape when the end of the reel is reached in high speed transport. It also allows frayed and wrinkled ends, which may cause uneven winds and damage recorder heads, to be removed without jeopardizing any recorded material. The free end of the tape should be secured with an appropriate pressure sensitive tape.

Handling large reels. Large reels should be handled and carried by the hub rather than the flange because a bent flange can damage the tape. The reel is removed from the transport by putting both hands as far around the back of the reel as possible. Do not push or pull the flanges.

Distortion and erasure of information. Care is required to prevent the accidental erasure of magnetic tapes. Magnetic fields which can emanate from transformers, motors, generators, bulk erasers, speakers, and other electric or electronic equipment may cause erasure. Fortunately, this problem occurs only in the vicinity of the magnetic field and depends on the strength of the field. Experts differ about the amount of separation needed—from three inches to two yards. Even the larger number can be easily accommodated in a library situation.

Accidental erasure of tape content may also result from the improper operation of equipment during playback. This can be avoided if the device that permits recording, e.g., tab, button, switch, is removed or turned off.

Vibrations can cause dropout or distortion in videotape. Videotapes should not be stored in an area where these are likely to occur.

Magnetic tape should not be placed on top of equipment in operation or until the equipment has cooled. For example, the heat generated by a sound tape machine may cause a temperature of 150°F (65°C), which is significantly higher than the 80°F (27°C) recommended as the upper temperature limit for good magnetic tape care. Heat can cause print-through in which one layer of tape transmits some of its information to an adjacent layer. Prompt removal of the tape from the machine at the end of the playback will decrease the chance of heat-induced print-through. Videotapes may suffer damage if placed on top of a color television set in operation because the magnetic fields associated with some components of the set may cause erasure of recorded signals.

Storage

All storage devices should be large enough to accommodate the container which houses a tape, cassette, or cartridge because a container provides necessary protection from dust and dirt. Some commercial storage units for sound and microcomputer cassettes, in particular, will not hold a container; these should be avoided unless they have a closing device which reduces the entrance of dust.

Magnetic tapes should be stored vertically because horizontal stacking can cause reel shape distortions in the lower part of the stack which, in turn, may damage the tape.

Intershelving of Magnetic Tape

Most videotapes can be successfully intershelved in the containers in which they have been received from commercial producers (Figure 1e) because these containers have been constructed so that the videotape is supported by the hub rather than the flange. Such containers are available commercially if needed. If a particular area of the library is subject to vibrations, a dummy block should be placed in the appropriate place on the shelf telling the patron where the item is housed. Reel-to-reel sound tapes in sturdy boxes are also easy to intershelve.

Sound cassettes and microcomputer cassettes present a shelving challenge due to their size. For this reason, the following suggestions apply mainly to them. Sound cartridges are mentioned peripherally only because few libraries possess them.

BOOK-LIKE ALBUMS (Figures 1d, 8, 28b)

Sound and microcomputer cassettes are ideally suited to storage in book-like albums because of their small, relatively flat shape. Albums commercially available in different sizes are able to house a varying number of cassettes; many such albums provide space for accompanying manuals. Preference should be given to those that accommodate the cassette container. Some of the most useful albums are among the cheapest; many of the more expensive are not designed to accept a container. Both types are illustrated in Figure 8.

A general description of book-like albums can be found in Chapter 4.

BOXES AND PAMPHLET BOXES (Figure 9)

Boxes and pamphlet boxes are particularly, but not exclusively, useful for sets containing seven or more sound or microcomputer cassettes. Pamphlet boxes rather than Princeton files are used for cassettes because the solid sides keep the cassettes well contained. Boxes may be homemade or purchased. Commercial corrugated cardboard boxes with inserts to hold cassettes are inexpensive and are available in different sizes. If a library has cassettes without cassette containers, storage in plastic bags which are then placed in closed containers may partially solve the dust problem.

A general discussion about boxes can be found in Chapter 4.

Figure 8. Book-like albums for sound or microcomputer cassettes housed with and without containers.

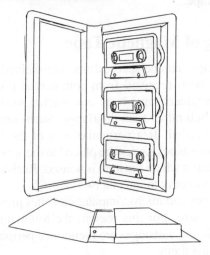

Figure 9. Commercial boxes for sound tapes are available in different sizes and materials.

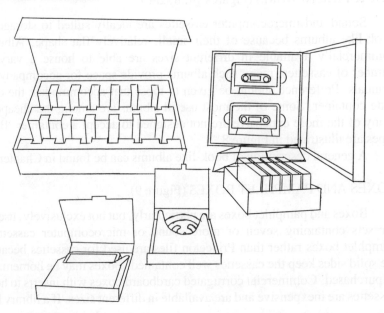

BINDERS (Figure 5c, 10)

Sound and microcomputer cassettes can be placed in the plastic "pages" of a binder. Preference should be given to plastic pages that can accommodate the cassette container. However, if the type of sound cassette page illustrated in Figure 10 is in use in the library, it can be inserted in a commercial or homemade transparent page normally associated with two-dimensional materials. This will provide protection against dirt and dust.

A general description of binders can be found in Chapter 4.

Figure 10. Binder with a sound cassette or microcomputer cassette page.

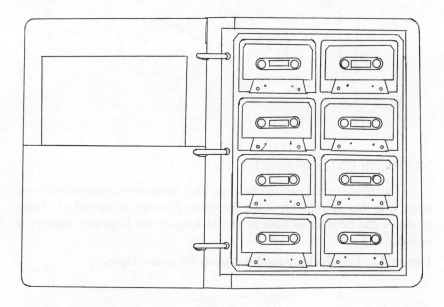

CLIP-ON HOLDERS (Figure 11a)

Reel-to-reel sound tapes, sound cassettes, and microcomputer cassettes can be housed in clip-on holders. The bigger holders will accommodate sets containing a limited number of pieces. The storage in the same unit of a number of cassettes which do not belong to one set should be avoided, because some cassettes will be pushed to the back, away from the notice of the browser.

Smaller holders are preferred for single items and two or three component sets. These shallow units will hold small items at the front of the shelf.

A general description of clip-on holders can be found in Chapter 4.

Figure 11. Some methods for intershelving sound tapes in which the individual labels are displayed.

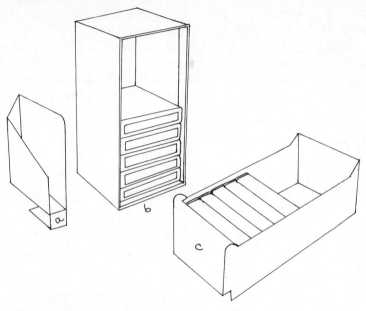

MODULAR UNITS (Figures 11b, 12)

There are several manufacturers selling inexpensive modules with one open side that permits browsing for either cassettes or cartridges. Some modules can be stacked with an interlocking device if greater capacity is needed.

Figure 12. Interlocking modular units for sound tapes.

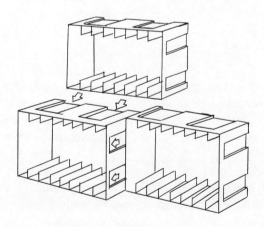

These units are another method of holding small cassettes and cartridges at the front of the shelf; they can accommodate a larger set than clip-on holders.

A general description of modular units can be found in Chapter 4.

TRAYS (Figure 11c)

Trays which house cassettes or cartridges may be less satisfactory than other storage methods because the labels on the cassettes or cartridges at the back of the tray may be difficult to read without removing the tray from the shelf.

Partial Intershelving of Magnetic Tapes

SHELF WITH COMMERCIAL RACK (Figure 5)

Racks designed to hold the various formats of magnetic tapes can be purchased and placed on one end of a shelf, or, if numbers warrant, a shelf-sized rack can be placed at the end of a particular classification sequence. Racks similar to the one illustrated in Figure 5 can house videotapes; smaller racks are available for cassettes and cartridges.

Less satisfactory is the rack standing outside the shelves because it removes the materials even farther away from their place in the general classification scheme. Such a rack should only be used when a library (a) already possesses the rack, (b) has a large number of cassettes in one general classification, e.g., the 780s, (c) can place the rack very close to the shelves containing other items with this classification.

HANGING DEVICES (Figure 6)

These devices described in Chapter 4 provide flexible storage which will accommodate cassettes, cartridges, and reel-to-reel sound tapes.

SEPARATE MEDIA SHELVES (Figure 13c & g)

Cassettes, cartridges, and small reel-to-reel sound tapes can be housed on the media shelves described in Chapter 4.

Figure 13. Separate media shelf.

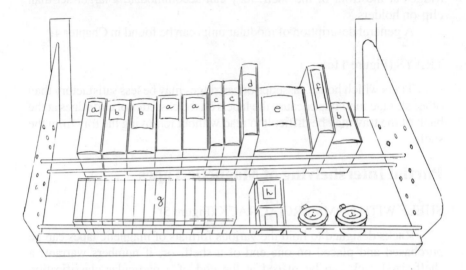

a. motion picture loop cartridge in container; b. microfilm reel in container; c. reel-to-reel sound tape in container; d. 8mm reel-to-reel motion picture in container; e. small model in box; f. small game in box; g. sound cassette in container; h. slides in semi-transparent box; i. filmstrip in canister

Chapter 7
Film Media (Filmstrips, Microforms, Motion Pictures, Slides, Transparencies)

Despite their different formats, all film media have many common guidelines for care and handling. The first section of this chapter deals with these common features. This is followed by sections devoted to the specific requirements for storage and, in some cases, care and handling of the separate film formats. The contents of this chapter are concerned with service copies; master copies should be preserved in archival conditions.

Photographs are not included in this chapter because most multimedia libraries do not circulate them. Some works about their care, handling, and storage are included in the bibliography.

Care and Handling

Handling Film. All film formats should be handled only at the edges, by the mounts, or by leader and end tapes. As with other nonbook materials, the oil and bacteria from fingerprints can cause deterioration and attract dust and dirt. The fingerprint itself is difficult to remove and will show on the item when it is projected. If touching the surface is unavoidable, clean lintless gloves should be worn.

Care should be taken not to twist or cinch film when handling. For example, the temptation to pull on the end of a filmstrip in order to fit it into a canister must be resisted because such cinching will cause scratches. Cinch marks may also appear if the film is dropped or jarred.

Film should be wound evenly in a tight roll without pulling. A roll which is not held firmly by its container should be fastened with a piece of special pressure sensitive tape, an acid-free button-and-string tie, or a sulphur-free rubber band.

Cleanliness. All film media must be kept clean. There is disagreement about whether film can be manually cleaned by someone other than an expert. This controversy can be explored by consulting the bibliography.

Dust is an enemy of film for it not only detracts from the picture image during projection, but it also causes film deterioration. Film should be stored in containers with lids which can be securely fastened, and equipment must be kept dust free. Do not blow on film to remove dust; moisture from the breath can condense on the film causing damage. A soft, dry brush or a can of clean pressurized air is recommended for removing dust from surfaces.

All film formats should be inspected after each use for dirt and damage, such as torn sprocket holes, weak splices, and tears. It is difficult to detect anything but the most obvious types of damage by manual inspection. Those libraries that do not have motion picture inspection machines and/or sufficient staff to inspect the other film media should encourage their patrons to report any damage or potential areas of trouble.

Heat and Humidity. Control of relative humidity in the environment is especially important for film. Dryness and dampness will both cause deterioration. An atmosphere with low humidity will result in brittle film which is easily destroyed. A damp sponge placed for a week with the film in an airtight container provides temporary relief by restoring brittle film, but the sponge must not touch the film.

On the other hand, high humidity encourages fungal growth and film base degeneration. The presence of Newton's Rings in slides indicates residual moisture and should alert the library to the possibility of high humidity levels. Silica gel placed in a container can be used to reduce moisture, but this is a temporary measure for it is no longer effective once its saturation point has been reached. Still film media can be dried by projection; however, each exposure must be limited to 30 seconds to prevent heat and light damage. In areas of high or low humidity, air conditioning is the only permanent solution.

While containers should be securely fastened to prevent the entrance of dust, they should not be airtight; the circulation of air prevents moisture accumulation.

High temperatures also contribute to the general deterioration of film. Therefore, film media should be stored away from sources of heat such as radiators, steampipes, hot air ducts, air conditioners, direct sunlight, and bright lights.

Color dyes are particularly subject to fading. However, the Eastman Kodak Company advertises that color film can be expected to have a useful life of many years if the film is shown with care and good projection equipment. The heat generated inside a projector can cause both color and black and white film to warp or even to melt. If a slide mounted in glass is subjected to such heat, the film can adhere to the glass. Only projectors with adequate cooling systems should be purchased. Care should be taken to use the correct wattage in the projection bulb. A higher than necessary wattage will produce added heat. Projection should be limited to 30 seconds for each slide or filmstrip frame or for each use of the stop button on a motion picture projector during normal viewing, as well as for drying out a too-humid film. Slides should not be left on light boxes, nor microforms in their readers, for prolonged periods. Film must be brought to room temperature before viewing. Sudden large temperature changes put great stress on film.

Composition of containers. Containers should be made of chemically stable plastic, acid-free cardboard, or non-ferrous metal, because these materials will not react with the chemicals in film. It is usually safe to use the containers in which film media are marketed because they are likely to be free of harmful ingredients.

Prohibited storage. The Eastman Kodak Company recommends that film not be stored near the following: ammonia, cleaners, formaldehyde, fungicides and insecticides, hydrogen sulfide, mercury, mothballs, motor exhaust, paints, solvents, turpentine, and wood glues. Storage on open shelves usually permits enough ventilation to minimize potential problems.

Integral magnetic sound. Motion pictures with magnetic sound tracks and sound slides will be governed also by the additional considerations for the care, handling, and storage of magnetic tape found in Chapter 6.

Filmstrips

Storage

Filmstrip canisters are small, lightweight, and, therefore, not easily intershelved by themselves. They are frequently sold with accompanying manuals with or without packaging. The filmstrip and manual should be stored together because a separately housed manual is more likely to be mislaid or lost, and the retrieval and shelving of separate parts involves twice as much work.

Filmslips are not included in this section because few libraries possess them. They should be treated in the same manner as filmstrips. Filmslips packaged in flat strips or produced in a rigid format are stored in the manner described for transparencies.

Intershelving of Filmstrips

BOXES AND PAMPHLET BOXES (Figures 1c, 14a, 17a, 22f)

Many filmstrips are sold in boxes suitable for intershelving. If a filmstrip with or without an accompanying manual is received in unsuitable packaging, both can be housed in a homemade, purchased, or casually acquired box. Commercial corrugated cardboard boxes with inserts to hold canisters are inexpensive and available in different sizes with capacities that range from 1 to 25 filmstrips. Most boxes enclose the filmstrip canister(s); there are some that are designed to expose the canister label (Figures 17a, 22f).

Pamphlet boxes rather than Princeton files are used for filmstrips because the canister's small size requires the confinement of solid sides. Pamphlet boxes should not be used in libraries where shelving might be done carelessly, e.g., where there are young, exuberant shelvers, because a canister may roll or be bumped out of a pamphlet box.

A general discussion about boxes can be found in Chapter 4.

BOOK-LIKE ALBUMS (Figures 14b, 28a)

Commercially produced book-like albums are available for single filmstrips or filmstrip sets. As with commercial boxes, some have windows or openings which allow the canister label to be seen.

A general description of book-like albums can be found in Chapter 4.

Figure 14. Commercial filmstrip containers.

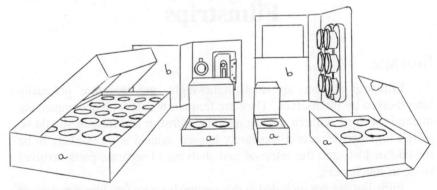

CLIP-ON FILMSTRIP CANISTER HOLDERS (Figures 4e, 17b & c)

The clip-on filmstrip holder is an effective device for libraries wishing to display canister labels. When holders are properly attached to the shelf, canisters are unlikely to fall out, yet they are easily removed. There are two types of holders, those that accommodate filmstrips only and those that house both filmstrip and manual. The holders are made with one, two, three, or four canister holes.

A general description of clip-on holders can be found in Chapter 4.

FREESTANDING CANISTER FILMSTRIP HOLDERS (Figures 15, 16b)

Freestanding tilted canister holders are similar to clip-ons in that they allow display of filmstrip labels and provide easy access. The commercially available holders, usually made of cardboard-like materials, are suitable only for filmstrips without manuals. These holders could be made of wood easily and economically by an amateur carpenter, e.g., staff member, volunteer, shop class student. There are advantages to the homemade holder; the required number of holes can be drilled and storage can be attached for manuals when needed.

TRAYS (Figure 17d)

Trays with inserts to hold filmstrip sets may not be as satisfactory as some other methods of storage because they do not accommodate manuals, and the canister labels at the back of the tray may be difficult to read without removing the tray from the shelf.

Figure 15. Homemade and commercially produced filmstrip canister holders.

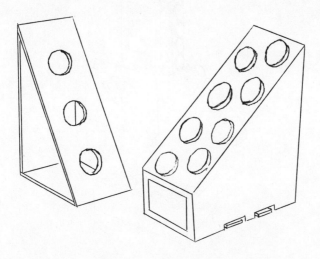

Figure 16. Freestanding tilted filmstrip holders used for total and partial intershelving.

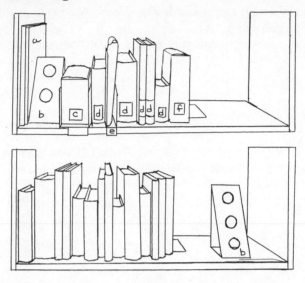

a. sound disc album in box; b. freestanding filmstrip canister holder; c. box containing microfilm placed in a clip-on holder; d. book; e. envelope containing two-dimensional material placed in a clip-on holder; f. microcomputer disks in box

Figure 17. Some devices for intershelving filmstrips in which individual canister labels are displayed.

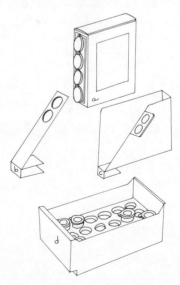

Partial Intershelving of Filmstrips

HANGING DEVICES (Figure 6)

These devices described in Chapter 4 can accommodate both film-strips and manuals.

SEPARATE MEDIA SHELF (Figure 13i)

Filmstrips without manuals can be housed on the media shelves described in Chapter 4.

Slides

Storage

This section on slide storage presupposes that all slides in the collection are mounted since this is the way most slides are purchased or returned from the film processor. Information concerning the selection of suitable mounts is found in works cited in the bibliography.

Some of the storage methods described below necessitate the handling of slides for projection. It is possible to fit each slide with an individual sleeve which gives added protection during handling and projection. This, of course, raises the cost of storage and must be weighed against the replacement value of the slide.

Intershelving of Slides

SLIDE TRAYS (Figure 1i)

Many slide sets are purchased or subsequently housed in slide trays which are designed to fit onto projection equipment. Some trays are received in boxes; others have storage lids. Both are easily intershelved. This method of storage is best suited to slides that will be used as a set because individual slides are not readily located.

Some librarians have adapted the slide trays so that only a staff member can insert or remove slides.

BOXES AND PAMPHLET BOXES (Figure 3d)

Boxes provided by manufacturers and processors make suitable storage containers because they are made of materials that will not harm the film. However, they are less than ideal for two reasons. First, each slide must be handled before it can be browsed or used. Second, most of these boxes are small and, therefore, may be overlooked if they are inadvertently pushed to the back of the shelf. These small boxes can be placed in larger containers or in pamphlet boxes; this is a solution for those with generous shelving space.

Camera stores sell boxes for slide storage, generally called slide files. The majority are rectangular and could easily be intershelved by placing the slide file on its side as long as it has a firm fastener that can withstand the hazards of shelving. Slide files have drawbacks also, because each slide must be handled for any type of use. If individual slides, rather than sets, are housed, the file must be well labelled for the retrieval of each slide.

A general discussion about boxes is found in Chapter 4.

CLIP-ON HOLDERS (Figure 4c)

Clip-on holders are another solution to the problem of small producers' boxes. Shallow holders will house these boxes at the front of the shelf. Tall, narrow clip-ons will accommodate plastic pages and envelopes of slides giving support to those that cannot stand vertically by themselves.

A general description of clip-on holders is found in Chapter 4.

BINDERS (Figure 1f)

Slides can be housed in the pockets of transparent inert plastic pages inserted in a binder. Semi-rigid plastic will protect the slides better than soft plastic because the page does not bend as readily or is not as likely to touch the surface of the film. Some more expensive pages have pockets that are molded so that air can circulate around both sides of every slide preventing moisture build-up. This method of storage allows easy intershelving and immediate browsing. However, slides must be handled for projection.

If the number of slides in a set is too large to be accommodated in a binder, the plastic pages can be housed in boxes, pamphlet boxes, or Princeton files.

A general description of binders is found in Chapter 4.

BOOK-LIKE ALBUMS (Figure 4d)

Book-like albums with permanently affixed boxes designed to hold slides are available. There are other albums which will hold slide carousels.

A general description of book-like albums is found in Chapter 4.

ENVELOPES (Figure 1j)

Single slides, Viewmaster, and other three-dimensional slides can be housed in acid-free, brightly colored manila envelopes. These envelopes can be intershelved or placed in the clip-on holders described above.

Partial Intershelving of Slides

HANGING DEVICES (Figure 6)

Plastic sheets of slides, slides stored in small producers' boxes, and single slides in an envelope made of acid-free paper can be housed in a plastic bag and stored by the methods described in Chapter 4.

SEPARATE MEDIA SHELVES (Figure 13h)

Only slides housed in small containers can be placed on the media shelves described in Chapter 4.

Microforms

Care and Handling

MICROFILMS

Open reels should not be filled because full reels are more difficult to handle, thereby increasing the possibility of damage. Microfilm should be stored on reels supplied by the manufacturer unless the reels are defective. If reels must be replaced or film is received without reels, microfilm should be placed on chlorine-free plastic reels.

Film on open reels is frequently secured with acid-free button-and-string ties. However, microfilm reels can be stored adequately without ties.

An 18-inch leader and tail will protect a microfilm against fingerprints, dust, and dirt.

MICROFICHES

Each microfiche may be housed in an acid-free paper envelope and stored vertically in one of the ways described below. This will protect the fiche and prevent it from sticking to another fiche. If proper temperature and humidity conditions can be maintained, it is possible to store them without the individual envelopes.

APERTURE CARDS AND MICROOPAQUES

Aperture cards and microopaques should be packed tightly so they will not warp. Acid-free inserts should be used in a container which is not full.

Intershelving of Microfilm Reels, Cartridges, and Cassettes

BOXES AND PAMPHLET BOXES (Figures 1k & l)

Most microfilms can be shelved in the boxes in which they are marketed. If these boxes are being pushed to the back of the shelf because of their small size, the stacking modules or clip-on holders described below will alleviate the problem.

Microfilm sets can be housed in boxes sized to appropriate dimensions, in pamphlet boxes, or in Princeton files.

A general discussion about boxes is found in Chapter 4.

CLIP-ON HOLDERS (Figure 16c)

Small clip-ons will hold one or two microfilms at the front of the shelf.

A general description of clip-on holders is found in Chapter 4.

MODULAR UNITS (Figure 3b)

Another method of holding microfilm to the front of the shelf is the use of modular units, which have one open side for browsing. Most of these inexpensive modules can accommodate four 16mm or two 35mm microfilms. Many units have an interlocking device for stacking if greater capacity is needed.

A general description of modular units is found in Chapter 4.

Intershelving of Microfiches, Microopaques, and Aperture Cards

BOXES AND PAMPHLET BOXES (Figure 22c)

Some sets of fiches, opaques, and cards are received in containers suitable for shelving; others can be placed in boxes or pamphlet boxes of appropriate sizes. Princeton files can only be used for large items which will not drop out of the bottom openings.

A general discussion about boxes is found in Chapter 4.

BINDERS (Figures 1b, 18)

The advent of the COM catalog has brought with it many commercially made sheet microform storage containers. Many of these are ring or album-type binders with pages especially adapted for microfiches so that the fiche header can be read without removing the item. The information on the fiche header may be easier to read if the binder is a different color than the fiche header.

This method of storage can also be used for microopaques and aperture cards if they are not too large to fit into the fiche pockets. The library staff could make pages for the larger items.

A general description of binders is found in Chapter 4.

Figure 18. Binder with microfiche pages.

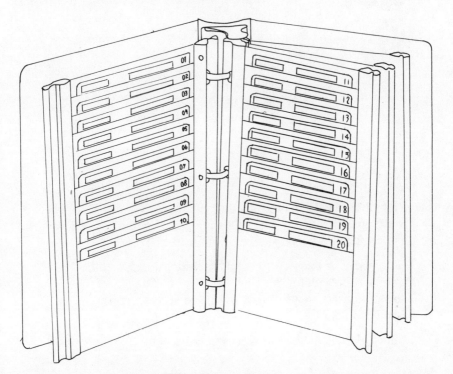

BOOK-LIKE CONTAINERS (Figure 19)

Each sheet of a microfiche, microopaque, or aperture card set may be inserted into a separate pocket of a book-like container. The number of pockets can be varied according to the size of the set. This container is easily intershelved.

Figure 19. Book-like containers for microfiche and microcomputer discs.

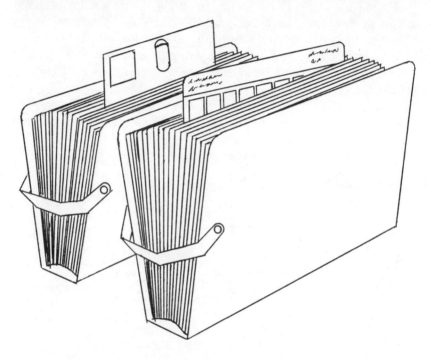

SINGLE ITEMS (Figures 3c, 28f)

Many librarians will not want to waste space by housing a single item in a box or pamphlet box. The following are suggestions for storing the single microfiche, microopaque, or aperture card:

1. The item can be housed in a large, brightly colored, acid-free envelope that is rigid enough for shelving.
2. The item can be housed in a binder page and the page placed in a pamphlet binder.

Either of these methods permits intershelving.

Partial Intershelving of Microforms

HANGING DEVICES (Figure 6)

These devices described in Chapter 4 can accommodate all formats of microforms.

SEPARATE MEDIA SHELF (Figure 13b)

Microfilms can be housed easily on the media shelves described in Chapter 4.

Motion Pictures

Care and Handling

REELS

Reels must be large enough to accommodate the film. It is recommended that a ¼-inch space for 8mm and a ½-inch space for 16mm be left between the film and the reel. Bent or rusty reels should be discarded.

Reels should be lifted by the hub or the lower flange to prevent damage to the edges of the film.

Only people who have proven their familiarity with motion picture projection should be allowed to run the equipment. They must be made aware that the equipment is never to be left during projection or rewinding and that the projector is to be stopped immediately if there are signs of trouble. Some types of equipment malfunctioning, e.g., scratching, can be discovered by running a length of black leader.

A five-foot leader and tail will help lessen the problems associated with dust, abrasion, and handling. A leader and tail of different colors can also help to distinguish the beginning from the end of the motion picture.

Storage

Motion pictures are marketed in cartridge, cassette, and reel formats. Cartridges and cassettes are usually packaged in a manner suitable for intershelving. Because they are designed for the layperson's use, they can tolerate normal library wear and tear.

Horizontal versus vertical storage for open reels is controversial because horizontal storage distributes the stress more evenly, but it is inconvenient for circulation. In addition, stacks of more than eight reels can cause too much stress on the bottom reels. The vertical storage of large films allows the whole weight to rest on the lower layers causing a distortion of the image. This is a lesser problem in active collections. Since easy access and an active collection are the premises of this book, the discussion will be confined to vertical storage.

Motion pictures should be stored no closer than six inches from the floor to reduce the incidence of dust and damage.

Intershelving of Motion Pictures

BOXES AND PAMPHLET BOXES (Figure 1h)

Any motion picture either received in a box or placed in a box which can stand upright by itself can be intershelved.

Because of their small size, motion picture loop cartridges may be pushed out of sight to the back of the shelf. These can be held at the front of the shelf by placing them in the clip-on holders or modular units described below. Cartridges can also be housed in boxes or pamphlet boxes.

There are boxes specially fitted for large motion picture reels, such as fast lock cases, which will hold the reel firmly. It is important that they be shelved in a manner that minimizes the possibility of falling over. This can be effected by the use of clip-on holders or wire bookends attached to the bottom of the upper shelf. Freestanding bookends are not advised because they can shift easily.

CLIP-ON HOLDERS (Figures 1g, 5e)

These holders solve two problems associated with motion picture storage. Shallow holders will house small size cartridges at the front of the shelf, and tall clip-ons will hold larger motion picture reels in an upright position.

A general description of clip-on holders will be found in Chapter 4.

MODULAR UNITS (Figure 16b)

Modular units with one open side for browsing are another method of holding motion picture loop cartridges at the front of the shelf. Most of these modules can accommodate two cartridges and have an interlocking device for stacking if greater capacity is required.

A general description of modular units is found in Chapter 4.

Partial Intershelving of Motion Pictures

MULTIMEDIA SHELVES WITH COMMERCIAL RACKS OR VERTICAL SLOTS (Figures 3f, 5f)

Motion pictures housed in film cans need individual support for vertical housing. This can be accomplished by placing racks at one end of a shelf or by building vertical slots. Movable racks and slots are advisable if the expansion and shifting of the collection is a possibility.

SEPARATE MEDIA SHELVES (Figures 13a & d)

Cartridges and small 8mm reels can be housed on the media shelves described in Chapter 4.

HANGING DEVICES (Figure 6)

Hanging bags can accommodate small reels and cartridges. However, the bags are not strong enough to store heavy film in metal containers.

A general description of hanging devices is found in Chapter 4.

CARTMOBILES (Figure 7)

Large reels can be stored on cartmobiles fitted with racks designed to hold the reels.

A general description of cartmobiles is found in Chapter 4.

Transparencies

Care and Handling

Transparencies do not require the same degree of attention to their care and handling as do filmstrips, motion pictures, and slides. The base on which the photographic image is placed is generally more durable, and the diazo dyes used on transparencies do not fade as easily as photographic dyes. In addition, the projection light is spread over a wider surface and is, therefore, less damaging.

Scratches and dust will show on the projected image, so it is wise to avoid these by housing transparencies in protective envelopes or folders and wiping them with a lint-free cloth after every use. A protective envelope with a window will facilitate browsing and decrease the amount of handling which always has a potential for damage.

Mounts are useful because they protect edges and prevent warping. Unmounted sets should have a sheet of acid-free paper between each transparency to protect them and prevent them from sticking together.

Storage

If the transparency mount is not strong or if the transparency is unmounted, it will buckle when shelved vertically. A rigid piece of cardboard or other material inserted in the protective envelope or folder will give support. All materials touching the transparency should be acid-free.

Transparencies should be stored in the same manner described for other two-dimensional materials in Chapter 8. These include:

- Envelopes (see also Figure 22b)
- Binders (see also Figure 3c). Three-ring binder pages specially adapted for transparencies can be purchased or made by the staff. Mounted transparency sets are sometimes housed in album-type binders because of their weight and bulk.
- Boxes and pamphlet boxes (see also Figure 22e)
- Multimedia shelf with movable spacing panels (see also Figure 3g)
- Multimedia shelf with pull-out racks or bins (see also Figure 4)
- Multimedia shelf with commercial rack (see also Figure 5)
- Hanging devices (see also Figure 6)

Chapter 8
Two-Dimensional Opaque Materials (Art Reproductions, Charts, Maps, Pictures, Postcards, Posters, Study Prints, Technical Drawings)

Some libraries circulate original works of art. In many instances the items belong to the artist who has an agreement with the library about their care, handling, storage, and circulation. Therefore, this chapter does not deal with two-dimensional original works of art, nor does Chapter 9 deal with three-dimensional works of art. Those libraries that own circulating original art collections are directed to the books in the bibliography.

Since postcards, posters, and technical drawings are found infrequently in multimedia collections, they are not mentioned specifically in this chapter. However, they have been added to the chapter's title because the considerations for care, handling, and storage outlined below apply to them as well as to other two-dimensional opaque materials.

Many two-dimensional opaque materials in circulating collections are relatively inexpensive or free, and some should be replaced frequently to keep the information up-to-date. Because most of these materials are made of paper which can be damaged easily, the staff must balance the costs of preservation against those of replacement. The following comments about care and handling should be considered with this in mind.

Care and Handling

Acid-free materials. Acid-free folders and acid-free interleaving sheets will help to lessen the inherent destructibility of paper because acid migrates from more to less acid paper. The interleaving sheets will also protect the surface of an item from the abrasion of friction when two or more items are housed in the same container.

Acrylic sprays. Acrylic spray can be used to protect and strengthen a sheet of paper. It also allows the sheet to retain its flexibility, if this is desired, and is relatively inexpensive. It is better to apply two or three thin coats rather than one thick coat.

Edging. Edging helps to prevent fraying and tearing. This inexpensive procedure can be done manually or with a simple-to-use, hand-operated machine which applies tape around the edges of a sheet of paper.

Cleanliness. Much surface soil can be removed by a soft rubber eraser.

Folding. If an item made of paper is received folded, a method of indicating the original manner of folding should be devised so that it will always be refolded in the same way. Folding against the folds already in the paper will weaken these areas.

If a decision is made to fold a large item for storage purposes, it is best if only a single fold is made with the grain of the paper. Particularly in maps the fold should be placed where it is least likely to affect important information because the fold area is subject to deterioration. All folds should be reinforced, especially at the intersection of fold lines. Adhesive cloth strips, tissues that are applied with water soluble adhesives or solvent activated adhesives, should be placed on areas of strain. Pressure sensitive tape should not be used because it will stain and damage paper.

An alternative method of folding (Figure 20) is to dissect the item into appropriately sized pieces, mount these pieces on a pressboard file folder

Figure 20.   Dissected map mounted on pressboard file folder.

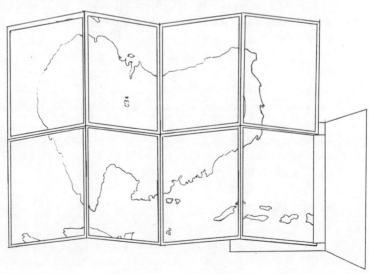

spaced to permit folding, and place the folded item into a pamphlet binder, an envelope, or other suitable container for storage. Pressboard file folders can be purchased or made by the staff.

Lamination. Lamination is expensive and should only be applied to items which have a high replacement cost and/or will be heavily used. Matte finish, which eliminates glare, is more expensive than gloss.

Lamination protects and strengthens materials, and its flexible nature stands up well to the hazards of circulation. It allows both sides of an item to be viewed, which is not possible with mounted materials. Seams in the laminate are subject to wear; it is important to buy laminate wide enough to cover the item. Large items should probably not be laminated because of the cost and the likelihood of seam wear.

Lamination will not prevent acidification; in fact, the heat of the press will speed up this process. If long term use is anticipated, paper should be deacidified before lamination. Lamination is not appropriate for archival materials because an image may be permanently altered by fixing it to plastic.

Mounting. Mounting also lengthens the active life of a picture or map. If a flexible mount is needed because of the method of storage, backings made of linen, pure rag paper, Wabasso cotton, or some other durable, nonacidic material are recommended. If the storage method requires the item to stand upright, the mount should be rigid enough to support the item but not so rigid that it will crack if subjected to pressure. The mount should be large enough so that there is a margin to absorb the wear and tear of handling and accommodate labels. Expert mounting can smooth out folds and wrinkles and make previous repairs less conspicuous. However, if damage occurs after the item is mounted, repairs are more difficult. Mounting is not suitable for two-sided items because one side will be permanently lost. Dry mounting, though more expensive than wet mounting, is recommended for items that will be part of a permanent collection because wet mounting may hasten the deterioration process. Information on mounting methods and materials is found in works cited in the bibliography.

An archival method which can be used for single-sided materials is to mount the item on an acid-free board which is hinged to a second board. A window is cut in the top board and filled with a polyester film. This holds the item firmly and allows browsing, but it does not withstand active circulation as well as some of the other types of protection.

Polyester encapsulation. Mounting and lamination are difficult to reverse and can cause some damage to the image if not carefully done. Another archival preservation method, called polyester encapsulation, which does not need expensive equipment or trained staff, seems preferable. The item is placed between two sheets of polyester cut two inches wider than its outside dimensions. The four edges are sealed with double sided adhesive tape after any air has been forced out of the envelope. This inexpensive protection allows both sides of an item to be seen.

Storage

It is possible to purchase some pictures and maps in protective plastic formats sometimes folded and with attached covers. These can be easily intershelved.

Two-dimensional opaque materials exist in a wide variety of sizes. Large items which cannot be conveniently folded to a size practical for shelving are discussed below under "Storage of Large Materials."

Intershelving of Two-Dimensional Opaque Materials

ENVELOPES (Figure 4b)

Inexpensive or ephemeral materials may not be worth the time and expense of the preservation methods mentioned under "Care and Handling." Such items can be stored in plastic or manila envelopes and intershelved. Large brightly colored envelopes will prevent their being overlooked in the search for information. If the envelope used is not rigid enough for shelving, a piece of stiff cardboard should supply the necessary support. Alternately the item can be stapled to a brightly colored manila folder and intershelved. Both envelopes and folders can be housed in one of the methods described below for added protection.

BOXES AND PAMPHLET BOXES (Figure 28h)

Several items with the same classification number can be housed in a box, pamphlet box, or Princeton file. These items should have sufficient protection so that they will not be crushed or torn during browsing and circulation. The box can either be circulated as a unit or each item can be provided with the paraphernalia necessary for individual circulation.

A general discussion about boxes can be found in Chapter 4.

CLIP-ON HOLDERS (Figure 16e)

Two-dimensional materials, either individually or in envelopes, which need support to stand vertically can be housed in clip-on holders. These steel units with their colorful epoxy finishes also attract attention to thin materials which can be overlooked easily.

A general description of clip-on holders can be found in Chapter 4.

BINDERS (Figures 1m, 5d, 21)

Single items can be housed in pamphlet binders which are available in several sizes. If the item is smaller than an open pamphlet binder, it can be attached at its mid-fold to the inner spine of the binder. An edge of a large single item can be attached to the inside of a pamphlet binder, and the item stored folded inside the binder.

Ring and album binders are suited to sets of two-dimensional materials because they can hold a varying number of pieces. Plastic pages designed to hold two-dimensional materials, and laminated, mounted, and encapsulated items with ring holes punched in their margins are stored in these binders and intershelved.

A general description of binders can be found in Chapter 4.

Figure 21. Binder containing pictures.

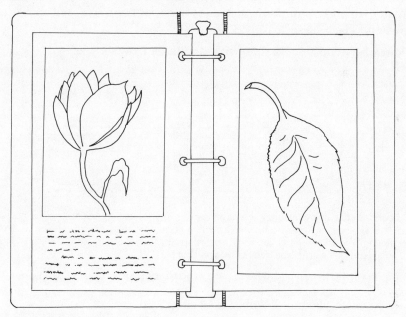

Partial Intershelving of Two-Dimensional Opaque Materials

MULTIMEDIA SHELF WITH MOVABLE SPACING PANELS (Figure 3h)

Items which can stand upright may be housed at the end of a shelf fitted with movable spacing panels. These can be placed wider apart than the measurement recommended for sound discs (see Chapter 5) because off-vertical stacking does not do the irreparable damage to two-dimensional opaque materials as it does to sound discs. If a library plans to house maps, pictures, transparencies, and sound discs together in vertical slots in a particular section of the collection, the panels should be three and one-half to four inches apart.

MULTIMEDIA SHELF WITH PULL OUT RACKS OR BINS
(Figure 22g)

This method is similar to that described for sound discs in Chapter 5. It is easier to browse the materials in the bin than in a rack; therefore, a bin is preferable because two-dimensional materials need not be held in the upright position required for sound discs. In order to utilize bins or racks, items must be the proper size, have some rigidity, or be in containers which provide support. A bin can be stationary if the position of the shelf allows its contents to be browsed easily.

Figure 22. Multimedia shelf with stationary browser bin.

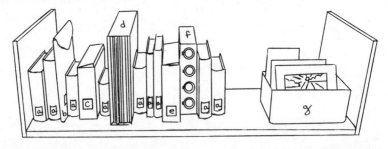

a. book; b. envelope containing a transparency; c. box containing microfiches; d. sound discs in slipcases in freestanding container; e. box containing transparencies; f. box containing filmstrips, sound cassettes, and manual; g. browser bin for two-dimensional materials (this bin can also be installed as a pull out bin)

MULTIMEDIA SHELF WITH COMMERCIAL RACK (Figure 5h)

Another method, described in Chapter 5, for shelving sound discs can be used to house fairly rigid two-dimensional materials of a suitable size.

HANGING DEVICES (Figure 6)

Two-dimensional materials that can fit, or be folded to fit, into a hanging bag (largest size 14 × 21 inches) are well suited to this type of storage. Many items may be browsed and circulated without removal from the bag.

A general description of hanging devices is found in Chapter 4.

Storage of Large Materials

A library with funding generous enough to provide much shelving space can intershelve all its materials, large and small, because it can devote one third, one half, or a whole shelf to one item. Most libraries are not as fortunate and must observe economy in shelving practice to a greater or lesser extent. In such cases, large size items must be housed elsewhere. However, a dummy should be placed in the classification sequence to indicate where the large item may be found, and the item should be stored as close as possible to the appropriate section of the collection.

Partial Intershelving of Large Two-Dimensional Materials

ROLLED STORAGE. (Figures 23, 24)

Experts disagree about whether rolled storage of large two-dimensional materials is advisable. Rolling and unrolling actively circulated items will undoubtedly cause deterioration. The seriousness of the deterioration is determined by the care exercised in handling. The following suggestions may help to alleviate some of the wear and tear.

- Items should always be rolled in the same direction and to the same diameter. If an item is received rolled, these factors should be noted.
- Items to be stored in a tube should be tied with a tape in a roll smaller in diameter than that of the tube, allowing the item to be easily removed

Figure 23. Roll storage.

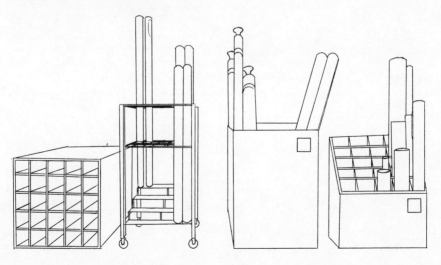

without tearing or fraying the edges. If for some reason it is difficult to remove the item, it is better to sacrifice the tube than to risk damaging the item.

- Items may be wrapped around the outside of a tube and covered with a sheet of protective material, such as polyester or acid-free paper. This method avoids the potential problems associated with insertion in and removal from tubes.
- Rolled items are difficult to browse. They should be well labelled with enough information so that the need to unroll and roll is reduced.
- The end of a cylinder, which rests on a hard surface when rolls are stored upright, can be subject to damage during shelving. For added protection of the contained material this cylinder end should extend one inch beyond the rolled edge of its contents.

Rolls can be stored in umbrella stands, racks intended for wine bottles, bins, cardboard boxes with partitions, as well as in traditional storage devices. Some libraries have installed cantilevered shelving or attached uprights to the front of the shelf to prevent rolls from falling. Others have affixed back-sloping pegs to walls to hold rolls.

Figure 24. Roll storage.

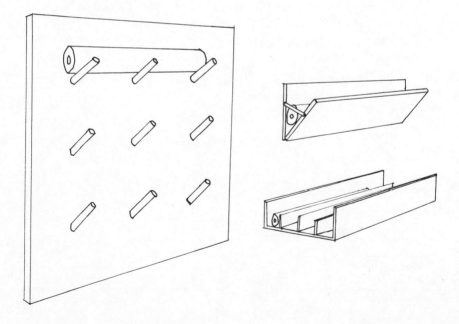

MOBILE STUDY PRINT BINS, ART PRINT UNITS, AND POSTER BINS (Figure 25)

Study prints are frequently produced on cardboard, which does not lend itself to folding or rolling. They are too large to be housed effectively on a standard shelf. These and other materials with similar dimensions can be stored in study print bins placed near the shelves with the appropriate classification. Mounted items which are too large for study print bins can be placed in poster bins or in art print shelving units.

It is not necessary that these bins be mobile, particularly if the shelving of the collection tends to be static. Mobility is useful with a growing collection.

Figure 25. Mobile units for the storage of large two-dimensional materials.

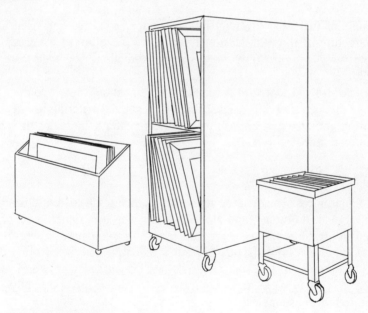

HANGING DEVICES

Large items can be hung from a freestanding rack or one attached to a wall at an appropriate height.

A general description of hanging devices is found in Chapter 4.

CARTMOBILES (Figure 7)

Large rigid items can be stored in racks placed on a cartmobile.

A general description of cartmobiles is found in Chapter 4.

Chapter 9
Three-Dimensional and Boxed Materials (Dioramas, Games, Globes, Kits, Models, Realia)

Because of the great diversity in size, shape, and materials used in the manufacture of three-dimensional and many-piece boxed materials, this chapter will provide only very general directions for their care and handling.

The size and awkward shape of some items should not discourage their storage on open shelving because three-dimensional materials usually draw attention and create interest in their subject matter. They may also attract potential patrons.

Care and Handling

Cleanliness. Dust can be reduced by placing transparent dust covers over models, dioramas, and globes when not in use. Other items can be stored in plastic bags which are then placed in a container. Three-dimensional materials should be dusted from time to time and wiped with a damp cloth to remove dirt. Some materials can be washed with warm, soapy water. It is preferable to use pure soap or detergents especially manufactured for museum use.

If an item is likely to attract insects, it should be sprayed once a year with an insect spray or powder.

Surface protection. Items which have painted or paper-covered surfaces can be coated with a clear polyurethane varnish. This will add protection and help the item to retain a "brand new" appearance. Other items, e.g., certain kinds of realia, can be protected by spraying them lightly with some forms of plastic.

Items with many parts. Boxed materials consisting of many parts can present an irritating problem. It seems inevitable that some parts will be lost and others placed in the wrong box. In a circulating collection this problem will never be completely solved. But it can be minimized. A inventory of the contents should be attached to the lid with a note asking the patron to check the contents before and after use and to report any missing part. This will help to make the patron aware of the need to "mind" the parts.

If it is feasible, all parts, including a dust cover, should be labelled. Unique call numbers may give sufficient identification.

Removable parts can be tied onto a basic model or globe or to a dust cover. If possible, the parts should be tied in such a way that the patron does not have to untie the parts in order to use the item.

Instructions can be copied when an item is received and spare copies kept filed by call number in a spare copy box in the workroom. Instructions on a single-sided sheet can be attached permanently to the container. One of the protective coverings described in Chapter 8 can be used to lengthen the life of an instruction sheet.

If pieces fit snugly into a container, and once removed are difficult to repack, a picture of the proper arrangement attached to the container may prevent damage from the forcing of parts.

Fragile materials. Some items of realia may be fragile. These should be mounted, displayed, or preserved in ways that will not destroy their usefulness. For example, a container housing seed samples must be moisture free. Delicate realia should not be able to move in the container. Padding can be added or a vial the exact size of the specimen selected as a container. A cicada picked up from a cottage floor and placed without preservatives in a transparent vial that fitted its dimensions survived intact the careless handling of 150 cataloging students, while a plastic skeleton commercially packaged in flimsy celluloid crumbled to pieces after being examined by 25 students.

Some experts advocate storage in light-tight containers because of the deteriorating effect light has on some items. Certain bottles and other containers used by the drug industry have been specially treated to block damaging rays. A Royal Ontario Museum staff member recommends the use of old-fashioned colored cellophane because it breathes and filters out some of the harmful light rays. The noise created when it is touched acts as a signal to an item's delicate nature. However, items in light-filtering containers cannot be viewed without removing them from the containers. The potential damage from light will have to be balanced against that from handling before a decision is made concerning transparent or light-filtering packaging for each item. My experience with many pieces of realia leads to the conclusion that proper packaging is a much more important preservation measure than protection against artificial light. The reason the cataloging class's cicada has remained intact for a number of years is that it is never removed from the vial, and there is no possibility of movement within it. It has never been exposed to sunlight; however, there appears to be no visible deterioration from many periods of two to three months in fluorescent classroom lighting.

Storage

There is more challenge in the effective shelving of three-dimensional materials than of any other type of material. There are fewer commercial products available to aid in their shelving, and very little has been written on the subject.

Intershelving of Three-Dimensional and Boxed Materials

BOXES AND BOX-LIKE CONTAINERS (Figures 1o, 4f, 5b, 22f, 26a, 28e)

Many items are sold in boxes designed for shelving. For example, some producers advertise "bookcase boxed games." Other manufacturers pare costs by using flimsy boxes. Some kits are marketed in boxes that are too large in relation to their contents. These waste space and/or overhang shelving. A general discussion about boxes and possible solutions to these problems is found in Chapter 4.

Figure 26.   Transparent containers.

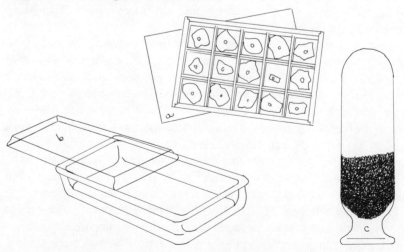

a. transparent tray; b. transparent box; c. transparent glass or plastic container.

TRAYS (Figure 26b)

Transparent plastic trays and similar containers, with and without lids, are commercially available, particularly from scientific suppliers. These are useful in housing small objects, e.g., a collection of minerals, the pieces of a reading readiness skill game, a model. Very small pieces should be kept in a plastic bag in the tray to minimize the chance of the loss of a part. Trays are easily intershelved.

UNUSUALLY SHAPED CONTAINERS (Figure 26c)

Containers with unusual shapes help to call attention to their contents.

CLIP-ON HOLDERS (Figure 4g)

A poorly packaged kit of two or three items can be housed in a clip-on holder. These units are sold in a variety of designs to accommodate filmstrips and/or sound tapes and/or shelf-size two-dimensional materials and/or motion picture loops and/or microfilms and manuals. Because these items are not housed in a container that will be circulated, they should be well labelled so that they can be reshelved easily.

A general description of clip-on holders is found in Chapter 4.

MODULAR SHELVING UNITS (Figure 27)

If a section of the classification contains many large three-dimensional and boxed items, it may be helpful to purchase modular shelving units with movable shelves which can accommodate unusual shapes. Some man-

Figure 27. Modular shelving units.

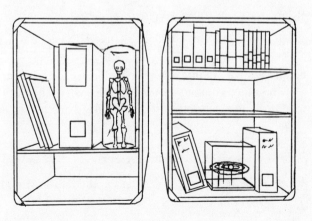

ufacturers market such shelving in lightweight, durable materials which can be shifted without back strain. An amateur carpenter on the staff may also provide innovative modules designed for the specific materials to be shelved.

Partial Intershelving of Three-Dimensional and Boxed Materials

MULTIMEDIA SHELF WITH STORAGE COMPARTMENTS (Figure 28)

Small items in trays, bags, or other transparent containers can be housed in a storage compartment placed on one end of a shelf. These compartments are marketed by scientific supply companies as "storage centers" or "display cases." They are enclosed on three sides with the open side facing the public and are divided into a number of cubicles which can house small containers.

Figure 28. Multimedia shelf with storage for small items.

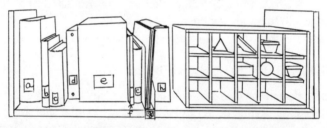

a. book-like album containing filmstrip set and manual; b. book-like album containing microcomputer cassettes; c. book; d. binder containing microcomputer disks; e. model in box; f. pamphlet binder containing a microfiche page; g. sound discs in slipcases in clip-on holder; h. box containing a set of maps

MULTIMEDIA SHELF WITH RACK (Figure 5i)

Boxed materials of a suitable size can be placed in racks which sit on one end of a shelf. The boxes should not be so large that they overhang the shelf by an appreciable amount, because the boxes can be damaged or the boxes and/or the other contents of the shelf thrown to the floor by a staff member or patron inadvertently hitting the overhang while passing the shelf.

SEPARATE MEDIA SHELF (Figure 13e & f)

Small boxed items can be stored on the media shelves described in Chapter 4.

HANGING DEVICES (Figure 6)

Hanging bags (discussed in Chapter 4) can accommodate many shapes, but they are limited in the size and weight of the items that can be housed in them.

Partial Intershelving of Large Size or Awkwardly Shaped Three-Dimensional and Boxed Materials

CARTMOBILES (Figures 7, 29)

Large and awkwardly shaped items can be housed on cartmobiles with flat shelves or those with racks.

A general description of cartmobiles is found in Chapter 4.

Figure 29. Cartmobile for large materials.

TABLES OR STANDS

An alternative to the expense of cartmobiles is to substitute a suitably sized table or stand which is not needed elsewhere. These should be placed as close to the appropriate section of the classification as possible.

UPPER AND LOWER SHELVES

Large and awkwardly shaped items can be placed on shelves that are too high or too low for the regular use of patrons. Very deep items can be housed here only if the shelving units are placed back to back with intervening partitions removed.

Even though the placement of less accessible shelves does not encourage, or in some cases permit, browsing, the size and general bright coloring of the items will attract the patrons' notice. In addition, a dummy placed in the appropriate classification sequence will also alert patrons to their existence. While not ideal, this shelving is better than having media housed unseen in the workroom.

Imaginative Shelving Ideas

A Toronto library stores items in steamer trunks, suitcases, briefcases, flight bags, refrigerator dishes, dishpans, clothes hampers, etc. The container is usually related to the contents, e.g., a wicker beach basket holds seashells and a pamphlet on life in the oceans. This packaging adds interest to the subject for the patrons and can be fun for the library staff who think up an appropriate container and then look for it at secondhand stores and rummage sales. This type of packaging does not require much money, only ingenuity and the right staff chemistry.

Chapter 10
Videodiscs

Videodiscs are new arrivals in the library world and many libraries have not yet added them to their collections. In part this is because the systems currently available for library use and those in development are incompatible. Libraries have adopted a "wait and see" stance, not wanting to commit resources until there is evidence that one or more systems will remain in production for the foreseeable future.

Because videodiscs are so new to libraries, little objective information on their care, handling, and storage is available. Producers and retailers of videodiscs are laudatory, naturally, describing them as "people-proof" and "care-free," and there are few libraries that have circulated them for an extended period of time. The many articles on videodiscs deal mainly with the mechanics of the different systems or the use of videodiscs in the library environment. The approach adopted here is tentative, and deals with two types of discs, the laser optical videodisc and the capacitance electronic disc.

LASER OPTICAL DISCS

The tracks of encoded information which comprise the 12-inch disc are encapsulated in a layer of transparent plastic. Some authorities claim that the disc surface is therefore immune to fingerprints and dust and that scratches will be virtually invisible in the pickup circuitry. Contrary opinions state that dust or scratches on the disc will cause intermittent scanning or failure to start, and they advise regular cleaning with a glass cleaner. Until it is clear which of these contrary opinions is correct, it is wise to clean the discs.

Everyone agrees that the player needs to be kept clean because dust on the lens will cause tracking problems. High humidity will also affect the proper functioning of equipment.

Because the scanning system does not touch the disc surface, the disc is not subject to wear and, theoretically, will last forever. It is, however, susceptible to warping and should be stored away from sources of heat. High humidity will cause labels to buckle which in turn will warp discs. Laser optical discs, made of a polymer formula, will also warp if stored vertically; they should be laid on a flat surface.

Horizontal storage is impractical in most intershelved collections because of the amount of space it requires and the nuisance of retrieving from, and reshelving into, a pile. I do not know of any commercially available devices for the partial intershelving of laser optical videodiscs. Figure 30 illustrates a device that would sit on a shelf in the appropriate classification section. This could be easily constructed by a staff member or local carpenter.

Figure 30. Unit for the storage of videodiscs.

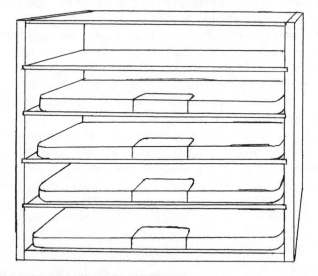

CAPACITANCE ELECTRONIC DISCS

The care, handling, and storage of the capacitance electronic disc is similar to that of the sound disc described in Chapter 5. However, these discs are not subject to quite the same hazards because they are enclosed by a protective sleeve called a caddy which is inserted into the player to both release and retrieve the disc before and after play. Under no circumstances should the disc be removed from the caddy when it is not in the player. Careless handling of the caddy is more likely when it is empty; care must be taken at all times to avoid bending the caddy. The opening of the caddy has strips of soft material that reduce dust entry and wipe the disc during insertion and retrieval. There is also an internal mechanism for cleaning the equipment's stylus. The result is a clean disc.

It is recommended that a new disc be played at normal speed without interruption at least once to condition the disc and ensure the reliable operation of the visual search function.

In personal conversations library staff who supervise the circulation of capacitance electronic discs and equipment report almost trouble-free performance so far. Occasionally, a patron returns the equipment with the disc jammed inside. This does not appear to affect the discs adversely.

Chapter 11
Microcomputer Disks

The advent of low-priced microcomputers has brought software to libraries. Microcomputer disks, called floppy disks, are plastic disks painted with a magnetic formulation.

Care and Handling

As far as care and handling are concerned they can be regarded as disk-shaped pieces of magnetic tape subject to the considerations outlined in Chapter 6.

The disk is permanently enclosed in a sleeve with only one access point open to receive a playback head. Fingers must be kept away from this open area because dirt and dust can seriously affect a disk's performance. Mason states that "Smokers may have more problems than nonsmokers. The thickness of a smoke particle exceeds the thickness of the recording media."[1]

In order to function properly a disk must be able to spin smoothly in its sleeve. Therefore, care must be taken to ensure that it neither bends nor warps.

Some manufacturers are producing sleeves that give more protection to a disk. For example, the Sony micro-floppy disk cover is made of rigid plastic with a sliding aluminum cover to protect the head window when the diskette is not in use. It is likely that the packaging of future formats of microcomputer disks will give better protection than many of those now on the market.

Extreme care should be exercised when writing on a disk label. Felt tip pens, rather than implements that require pressure such as pencils or ball point pens, should be used.

Storage

Microcomputer disks can be stored in many of the ways described for two-dimensional materials in Chapter 8 with sufficient protection to prevent bending or warping. These include:

- Envelopes. Envelopes that contain disks must have rigid inserts to protect the disk from the possibility of being bent. Each disk should be placed in its own dust jacket or sleeve. However, several of these sleeves can be housed in the same envelope.
- Binders (see also Figure 28d). Vinyl pages that hold microcomputer disks are available commercially for both ring and album binders.
- Boxes and pamphlet boxes.
- Clip-on holders.
- Multimedia shelf with rack or bin.
- Hanging device (see also Figure 6).

Microcomputer disks can also be inserted into individual pockets bound together into a book-like container (Figure 19).

Library supply firms are developing containers for microcomputer disks suitable to open access shelving. A variety of packaging is likely to become available as more collections include this type of material.

Reference

1. Robert M. Mason, "All About Diskettes," *Library Journal,* vol. 109, no. 5 (March 15, 1984): 559.

Bibliography

This bibliography contains not only works that pertain to information contained in the text but also citations of subject matter outside its scope. The latter have been included to help library staff find information on particular aspects of the care, handling, and storage of media which have either been omitted or not fully discussed in this book, e.g., archival preservation.

There are many books and articles on some subjects, such as the care of slides. The ones chosen for this bibliography are library-oriented except in a few cases where the information contained is of particular interest.

A decision was made to include only items published from 1975 on. Items sent to me by producers and publishers as the most up-to-date treatment of a subject are included although they were published before 1975; this is indicated by placing the date of receipt or printing in parentheses after the date of publication. Several bibliographies have been added to this bibliography for those searching for earlier titles.

Some works are listed here even though they contain only a brief overview of a subject.

Abbott, Andrew D., Jr., and Salesi, Rosemary A. "Preserve Your Media Collection Today." *Audiovisual Instruction* 24 (6) (September 1979): 29–31.

The effect of environmental facts on all media, including a chart that shows the changes caused by different temperatures and relative humidities.

Alexandrovich, George. "Keeping It Clean: Record Hygiene." *Stereo Review* 42 (6) (June 1979): 78–81.

The results of stylus and sound disc wear and disc cleaning are examined using a scanning electron microscope.

American National Standards Institute. *American National Standard Practice for Storage of Processed Safety Photographic Film.* Rev. ANSI PH.1 43-1979. New York: ANSI, 1979.

These standards discuss the care, handling, and storage of still film, motion pictures, and microforms in medium term and archival collections.

Association for Library Service to Children. Print and Poster Evaluation Committee. *Developing and Managing a Print and Poster Collection for Children*. Chicago: ALSC, n.d.

Includes an overview of surface protection, mounting, framing, circulation procedures, display, and storage.

Avedon, Don M. "The More Practical Microfilm—Vesicular." *Library Resources & Technical Services* 24 (4) (Fall 1980): 325–28.

A brief guide to the care, cleaning, and storage of vesicular microfilm.

Bahr, Alice Harrison. *Microforms: The Librarians' View, 1978-79*. The Professional Librarian Series. White Plains, NY: Knowledge Industry Publications, 1978.

Pages 58–63 give a brief review of research, studies, and standards on the care and storage of microforms.

Banks, Joyce M. *Guidelines for Preventative Conservation*. Ottawa, ON: Council of Federal Libraries, Committee on Conservation/Preservation of Library Materials, 1981.

This pamphlet in English and French on guidelines for archival collections includes microforms.

Bartlett, James, and Marshall, Douglas. *Maps in the Small Historical Society: Care and Cataloging*. Technical Leaflet, No. 111; History News, Vol. 34, No. 1. Nashville, TN: American Association for State and Local History, 1979.

A brief introduction to storage in archival collections.

Basic Preservation Procedures. SPEC Kit, No. 70. Washington, DC: Systems and Procedures Exchange Center, 1981.

For archival collections. On pages 52–57 are the Newbery Library's instructions for matting and framing art objects on paper; pages 60–62 contain the Stanford University Libraries' encapsulation procedures; pages 78–85 have Yale University's guidelines for the physical handling and storage of microforms.

Bateman, Robin. "Integrated Multi-media Libraries: At What Stage the Integration?" *The Audiovisual Librarian* 6 (2) (1980): 16–20 and Payne, Bruce. "Letters." *The Audiovisual Librarian* 6 (2) (1980): 63–64 and Power, John. "Letters." *The Audiovisual Librarian* 6 (4) (1980): 137.

The concept of intershelving is opposed in the article and upheld in the letters.

Beatty, LaMond F. *Filmstrips*. The Instructional Media Library, No. 4. Englewood Cliffs, NJ: Educational Technology, 1981.

Pages 75–79 have step-by-step illustrated instructions for splicing filmstrips. Very little on care, handling, and storage.

Boss, Richard W., with Raikes, Deborah. *Developing Microform Reading Facilities*. Microform Review Series in Library Micrographics Management, No. 7. Westport, CT: Microform Review, n.d.

Practical, readable, well illustrated. Discusses the care and storage of film, fiche, ultrafiche, and microopaques.

Bow, Eric C., comp. *Index to Canadian Library Supplies*. 3d ed. Toronto, ON: Ontario Ministry of Culture and Recreation, Information Access Division, Libraries and Community Information Branch, 1980. Free.

Suppliers are listed alphabetically. Includes product index.

Brown, Margaret R., with the assistance of Etherington, Don, and Ogden, Linda K. *Boxes for the Protection of Rare Books: Their Design & Construction*. A National Preservation Program Publication. Washington, DC: Library of Congress, 1982.

Well illustrated, step-by-step instructions for archival boxes which can have applications for the construction of containers for nonbook materials.

Care and Handling of Magnetic Tape. Redwood City, CA: Ampex, 1976 (received 1982). Free.

Ampex distributes this pamphlet as their official advice on care and handling. The emphasis is on videotapes; there is very little material on storage.

The Care of Video Cassettes. Technical Information, No. 3. The Hague: International Council for Educational Media, 1980. Free.

A nontechnical pamphlet in English, French, and German about care and handling; little information about storage.

Casciero, Albert J., and Roney, Raymond G. *Introduction to AV for Technical Assistants*. Littleton, CO: Libraries Unlimited, 1981.

Includes labelling of software, care of equipment, mounting techniques, and one or two lines on the storage of each type of material discussed. Many pictures and diagrams.

Chibnall, Bernard. *The Organisation of Media*. London: C. Bingley, 1976.

Pages 55–58 contain a general discussion about storage.

Cluff, E. Dale. *Microforms*. The Instructional Media Library, No. 7. Englewood Cliffs, NJ: Educational Technology Publications, 1981.

Pages 42–48 give a brief overview of specialized, nonarchival collections.

Cunha, George M.; Lowell, Howard P.; and Schnare, Robert E. *Conservation Survey Manual*. [S.1.]: Section on the Management of Information Resources and Technology of the New York Library Association, 1982.

Pages 31–40 discuss surface cleaning, paper repair including a recipe for past, and polyester film encapsulation with illustrations.

Cunha, George Martin, and Cunha, Dorothy Grant. *Library and Archives Conservation: 1980s and Beyond*. 2 vols. Metuchen, NJ: Scarecrow, 1983.

Principally concerned about the long term preservation of paper materials, this work has a few pages devoted to nonprint materials. Its value for circulating collections lies in its extensive bibliography which fills the second volume.

Daniel, Evelyn H., with Stiles, Karen A. *Media in the Library: A Selected, Annotated Bibliography*. Syracuse, NY: ERIC Clearinghouse on Information Resources, Syracuse University, 1978.

Some of these approximately 500 titles (most with annotations) deal with care, handling, and storage of various media.

Darling, Pamela W. ''Microforms in Libraries: Preservation and Storage.'' *Microform Review* 5 (2) (April 1976): 93–100.

Contains criteria for decisions as to suitable subject content for different microform formats and proper methods for the care and handling of master and service copies.

Davidson-Arnott, Frances, comp. *Policies and Guidelines Developed for Community and Technical College Libraries*. Ottawa, ON: Canadian Library Association, 1983.

Pages 5–45 present eight institutions' contributed statements dealing with the circulation of hardware and software.

Davies, Helen. ''Storage of Audio-visual Materials in the Library.'' *Assistant Librarian* 69 (1) (January 1976): 6–8.

A survey of AV shelving and packaging suppliers in Britain. Though out-of-date it may provide leads to items currently available.

Diaz, Albert James, ed. *Microforms in Libraries; A Reader*. Weston, CT: Microform Review, 1975.

Pages 174–76 and 234–56 deal with environmental conditions, archival storage, and security. Includes some mention of open storage.

Dobbin, Peter. "Laser Disc and Magnavision Video Disc Players: A Matter of Tempered Excitement." *Modern Photography* 44 (12) (December 1980): A7-A9, A15.

Comments on the care and handling of optical videodiscs and playback equipment.

Donnelly, Arthur R. "Multimedia Integrated Shelving: A Survey of Its Use in Academic Libraries of the Southeast with Guidelines for Implementation." EdD dissertation, George Peabody College for Teachers, 1978. Ann Arbor, MI: University Microfilms, 1979. Microfilm.

The results of a survey of 39 institutions led to this list of 21 guidelines for the implementation of intershelving.

Dove, Jack. *The Audiovisual: The Availability and Exploitation of Nonprint Material with Specific Reference to Libraries*. London: A. Deutsch, 1975.

Pages 242–45 give a brief overview of care and storage, with some methods for intershelving mentioned.

Drazniowsky, Roman, comp. *Map Librarianship: Readings*. Metuchen, NJ: Scarecrow, 1975.

Pages 359–410 include five articles originally published elsewhere between 1961 and 1972 which discuss various aspects of storage and preservation.

Duane, James E. *Media about Media: An Annotated Listing of Media Software*. The Instructional Media Library, 6. Englewood Cliffs, NJ: Educational Technology Publications, 1981.

Approximately 400 annotated audiovisual works, mostly produced in the 1970s, deal with a wide range of media topics, including equipment operation, displays, mounting, and various nonbook materials.

Edridge, Sally, ed. *Non-book Materials in Libraries: Guidelines for Library Practice*. Wellington: New Zealand Library Association, 1980.

This concise overview of the organization of art originals, art reproductions, charts, filmstrips, kits, maps, microforms, photographs, pictures, posters, slides, sound recordings, technical drawings, transparencies, and videotapes includes a brief discussion of closed access and total and partial integration followed by recommendations for the care and storage of each medium.

Ehrenberg, Ralph E. *Archives & Manuscripts: Maps and Architectural Drawings*. SMA Basic Manual Series. Chicago: Society of American Archivists, 1982.

Pages 42–52 deal with archival storage and conservation including flattening, surface cleaning, mending, reinforcement, neutralization and buffering, polyester film encapsulation, matting, and framing.

Ellison, John W.; Gerber, Gloria S.; and Ledder, Susan E. *The Storage and Care of Films, Filmstrips, Filmloops, Transparencies, & Slides*. Buffalo, NY: School of Information and Library Studies, State University of New York, 1978–79; distributed by National Audiovisual Center, Washington, DC. 75 slides, 1 sound cassette.

Gives general principles of care and handling for all film media; the storage of motion pictures and slides in active collections. The storage of filmstrips, filmloops, and transparencies is not discussed.

―――――. *The Storage and Care of Magnetic Tape (Audio, Video & Computer)*. Buffalo, NY: School of Information and Library Studies, State University of New York, 1978–79; distributed by National Audiovisual Center, Washington, DC. 77 slides, 1 sound cassette.

Primarily concerned with care and handling in active collections, including those that are intershelved.

―――――. *The Storage and Care of Maps*. Buffalo, NY: School of Information and Library Studies, State University of New York, 1978–79; Distributed by National Audiovisual Center, Washington, DC. 69 slides, 1 sound cassette.

Primarily concerned with the care, handling, and storage in active collections. Intershelving is not considered.

―――――. *The Storage and Care of Microforms (Films, Fiche, & Ultrafiche)*. Buffalo, NY: School of Information and Library Studies, State University of New York, 1978–79; distributed by National Audiovisual Center, Washington, DC. 66 slides, 1 sound cassette.

Discusses care and handling, and to a lesser extent storage, in active collections of microforms on silver halide, diazo, and vesicular film.

―――――. *The Storage and Care of Phonorecords*. Buffalo, NY: School of Information and Library Studies, State University of New York, 1978–79; distributed by National Audiovisual Center, Washington, DC. 68 slides, 1 sound cassette.

Although this is presented as a discussion about active collections, its viewpoint is conservative, particularly in regard to storage. Good coverage of care and handling.

————. *The Storage and Care of Photographs and Negatives*. Buffalo, NY: School of Information and Library Studies, State University of New York, 1978–79; distributed by National Audiovisual Center, Washington, DC. 65 slides, 1 sound cassette.

Deals with care, handling, and storage in active collections.

Ellison, John W.; Gerber, Gloria S.; and Sandner, Fred. "How to Care for Your Films." *Instructional Innovator* 26 (2) (Feburary 1981): 36–37.

A discussion of the care and handling and some storage of all film formats.

Ellison, John W., et al. "Storage and Conservation of Microforms." *Microform Review* 10 (2) (Spring 1981): 90–93.

This rewriting and slight enlargement of the sound cassette script listed in #38 (above) has a different optimum for relative humidity.

Evans, Hilary. *Picture Librarianship*. Outline of Modern Librarianship. New York: K. G. Saur, 1980.

Pages 40–60 consider special collections—the care and handling of prints, engravings, photographs, negatives, and slides in archival collections; the advantages and disadvantages of mounting; mounting methods; open and closed access; some suggestions for storage.

Folcarelli, Ralph J.; Tannenbaum, Arthur C.; and Ferragams, Ralph C. *The Microform Connection; A Basic Guide for Libraries*. New York: Bowker, 1982.

Includes information on cleaning and splicing, a checklist for care and handling, and a brief discussion of storage methods.

Ford, Karin E. "Idaho Conservation: The Preservation of Photographs." *The Idaho Librarian* 35 (3) (July 1982): 110–12.

Summarizes, in lay language, the care and handling of color and black and white photographs, with suggestions for storage containers.

Fothergill, Richard, and Butchart, Ian. *Non-book Materials in Libraries: A Practical Guide*. London: C. Bingley, 1978.

Pages 198–207 have an overview of the intershelving of portfolios containing paper or photographic prints, slides, filmstrips, microforms, motion pictures, sound tapes, sound discs, and transparencies, with particular emphasis on labelling.

Funk, Grace E. "Where Do I Look for It? On the Mechanics of an Integrated Collection." *Bookmark* 16 (5) (January 1975): 13–17.

Offers practical suggestions for intershelving.

Gerber, Gloria S., et al. "Map Storage and Care in Active Collections." *Special Libraries Association Geography and Map Division Bulletin* 125 (September 1981): 15–18.

Gives a condensation of the sound cassette script listed in #37 (above).

Griffin, Marie P. "Jazz at Rutgers." *Conservation Administration News* 10 (July 1982): 6–8.

Contains a concise description of the archival care and storage of 16, 33⅓, 45, and 78 rpm recordings, cylinders, and piano rolls and the maintenance of related equipment.

Guldbeck, Per E. *The Care of Historical Collections; A Conservation Handbook for the Nonspecialist*. Nashville, TN: American Association for State and Local History, 1972 (1982 printing).

Written with clear instructions for the small historical society or museum, this book includes the conservation of paper, wood, leather, metals and alloys, textiles, ceramics, and an appendix on adhesives.

Halsey, Richard Sweeney. *Classical Music Recordings for Home and Library*. Chicago: American Library Association, 1976.

Pages 272–77 include problems originating in the factory; poorly maintained or inadequate equipment; user handling; environmental conditions; a review of various methods of cleaning discs.

Handling and Storage of Magnetic Recording Tape. St. Paul, MN: 3M, n.d. Free.

This pamphlet is written in nontechnical language about the care, handling, and long term storage with an emphasis on videotapes.

Handling, Repair, and Storage of 16mm. Motion Picture Films. Lincolnwood, IL: Research Technology, 1977.

This pamphlet includes a fairly detailed discussion of cleaning and lubricating fluids, splicing, and automatic electronic inspection equipment.

Harrison, Alice W. *The Conservation of Library Materials*. Dalhousie University School of Library Service Occasional Paper, 28. Halifax: Dalhousie School of Library Service, 1981.

A discussion of the main points culled from many works about the preservation of paper. Canadian, American, and some British sources of archival supplies are given.

Harrison, Alice W.; Collister, Edward A.; and Willis, R. Ellen. *The Conservation of Archival and Library Materials: A Resource Guide to Audiovisual Aids*. Metuchen, NJ: Scarecrow, 1982.

An annotated bibliography of approximately 500 audiovisual works produced between 1955 and 1980 arranged by title with a subject index.

Harrison, Helen P., ed. *Picture Librarianship*. Phoenix, AZ: Oryx Press, 1981.

Pages 65–130 include essays about the care, handling, and storage of photographs, negatives, illustrations, slides and to a limited extent microforms, filmstrips, and transparencies; detailed discussion about mounting techniques and the advantages and disadvantages of mounting. Archival collections stressed, but some attention paid to user collections and intershelving.

Hart, Thomas L. "Dare to Integrate." *Audiovisual Instruction* 21 (8) (October 1976): 18–19.

The author refutes arguments frequently used to condemn intershelving and briefly examines the positive experiences of two school media centers.

Hart, Thomas L., comp. and ed. "Integrated Shelving of Multimedia Collections." *School Media Quarterly* 5 (1) (Fall 1976): 19–30.

Sara L. Buckmaster, Clara Thoren Rottman, Arabelle Grant, Patricia B. McCarthy, and Helen Laleiki contribute articles on their positive experiences with intershelving.

Hektoen, Faith H., and Rinehart, Jeanne R., eds. *Toys to Go: A Guide to the Use of Realia in Public Libraries*. Chicago: American Library Association, 1976.

Includes circulating procedures and a chart on the advantages and disadvantages of various containers and devices.

Henderson, Kathryn Luther, and Henderson, William T., eds. *Conserving and Preserving Library Materials*. Allerton Park Institute, 27. Urbana, IL: University of Illinois Graduate School of Library and Information Science, 1983.

Papers delivered at an institute on archival preservation include "Preservation of Paper Based Materials: Mass Deacidification Methods and Projects"; "Preservation of Paper Based Materials: Present and Future Research and Developments in the Paper Industry"; and "Preservation of Nonpaper Materials: Present and Future Research and Development in the Preservation of Film, Sound Recordings, Tapes, Computer Records, and Other Nonpaper Materials."

Hess, Stanley W. *An Annotated Bibliography of Slide Library Literature*. Bibliographic Studies, No. 3. Syracuse, NY: Syracuse University School of Information Studies, 1978.

Pages 24–25 list 6 items published between 1965 and 1977 on the care and preservation of films and slides.

Hoffman, Frank W. *The Development of Library Collections of Sound Recordings.* Books in Library and Information Science. New York: M. Dekker, 1979.

Pages 80–90 contain a good discussion of cleaning methods and products; pros and cons of open access; problems of ensuring proper care of circulating items.

Hohenstein, Margaret, et al. *Cataloging, Processing, Administering AV Materials: A Model for Wisconsin Schools.* 3d rev. ed. Madison, WI: Wisconsin Library Association, 1981.

Includes brief instructions for the care and intershelving of a wide range of media. Useful illustrated directions for processing materials for circulation.

Hyman, Richard. *Shelf Access in Libraries.* ALA Studies in Librarianship, No. 9. Chicago: American Library Association, 1982.

The author argues against intershelving in a general discussion of shelving in various types of libraries.

————. *Shelf Classification Research: Past, Present—Future?* University of Illinois Graduate School of Library Science Occasional Papers, No. 146. Urbana, IL: University of Illinois, 1980.

Pages 25–29 give brief comments on the statements of five librarians about intershelving.

Irvine, Betty Jo, with the assistance of Fry, P. Eileen. *Slide Libraries: A Guide for Academic Institutions, Museums, and Special Collections.* 2d ed. Littleton, CO: Libraries Unlimited, 1979.

Pages 166–87 discuss different types of storage facilities ranging from closed storage to intershelving. Includes citations for other works and institutions where particular systems are used. This is followed by a survey of works about environmental controls. Pages 223–28 have a detailed description of mounts.

Jonassen, David H. *Nonbook Media: A Self-paced Instructional Handbook for Teachers and Library Personnel.* Hamden, CT: Library Professional Publication, 1982.

Simple instructions with illustrations and a bibliography for rubber cement mounting and dry mounting (pp. 115–23) and film splicing (pp. 257–61).

Jones, Craig. *16mm Motion Picture Film Maintenance Manual.* Consortium of University Film Centers Monograph Series, 1. Dubuque, IA: Kendall/Hunt, 1983.

A well illustrated, detailed description of film damage, repair, and damage prevention together with an overview of storage.

Keck, Caroline K. *A Handbook on the Care of Paintings*. Rev. ed. Nashville, TN: American Association for State and Local History, 1976.

A description of the anatomy, conservation, and restoration of paintings with a brief discussion about archival storage.

————. *How to Take Care of Your Paintings*. 2d ed. New York: Scribner, 1978.

A very practical, easy-to-read discussion about the cleaning, repair, and safe transportation of paintings with some reference to prints and watercolors. Simple line drawings illustrate the text.

Kidd, Betty. "Preventive Conservation for Map Collections." *Special Libraries* 71 (12) (December 1980): 529–38.

Discusses environmental problems, conservation, and storage for archival collections, researcher's agreement for National Map Collection, Public Archives of Canada.

Kogan, Marilyn H., and Whalen, George. *Organizing the School Library: A Canadian Handbook*. Toronto, ON: McGraw-Hill Ryerson, 1980.

Pages 218, 223–25 have brief suggestions for shelving including intershelving.

Korty, Margaret Barton. *Audio-visual Materials in the Church Library: How to Select, Catalog, Process, Store, Circulate, and Promote*. Riverdale, MD: Church Library Council, 1977.

Suggestions for the intershelving and/or partial intershelving of filmstrips, slides, motion pictures, sound recordings, transparencies, stereographs, pictures, and maps, and for the mounting and reinforcement of pictures and maps.

Kyle, Hedi. *Library Materials Preservation Manual: Practical Methods for Preserving Books, Pamphlets, and Other Printed Materials*. Bronxville, NY: N.T. Smith, 1983.

Well illustrated with step-by-step instructions, this work includes information on the proper set-up of work areas, adhesives, folding, edge cutting, knots, the construction of pamphlet binders, and the cleaning and repair of paper.

Langrehr, John S., and Russell, Anne. "Audiovisual Packaging and Shelving." *Audiovisual Instruction* 22 (9) (November 1977): 12–14.

Gives a detailed description of a packaging system suitable for intershelving developed by an Australian library.

Larsgaard, Mary. *Map Librarianship: An Introduction*. Littleton, CO: Libraries Unlimited, 1978.

Pages 155–87 include a practical, easy-to-read discussion about environmental problems, handling, care, repair, and storage of maps with references to other sources throughout the text. Brief mention of globes.

Le Clercq, Angie. "Videodisc Technology: Equipment, Software, and Educational Applications." *Library Technology Reports* 17 (4) (July-August 1981): 293–334.

This study of the MCA/DVA/Pioneer/Magnavox laser optical system and the RCA/Zenith/CBS capacitance system includes a brief discussion of the care of equipment and the care, handling, and storage of software.

Library of Congress. Preservation Office. *Newsprint and Its Preservation.* Rev. ed. Preservation Leaflet, No. 5. Washington, DC: Library of Congress, 1981. Free.

A concise description of the archival care and handling of newspaper clippings.

————. *Polyester Film Encapsulation.* LC Publications on Conservation of Library Materials. Washington, DC: Library of Congress, 1980.

Provides step-by-step illustrated instructions for making a basic polyester envelope.

————. *Preservation of Library Materials: First Sources.* 3d ed. Preservation Leaflet, No. 1. Washington, D.C: Library of Congress, 1982. Free.

This annotated bibliography which emphasizes the archival preservation of books includes citations for other media.

"LJ's Annual Buyers' Guide." *Library Journal* and "SLJ Annual Buyers' Guide." *School Library Journal.*

The same list of firms with a product index is published in a selected issue annually in both periodicals. Contact *Library Journal* and/or *School Library Journal* for information.

McCarthy, Patricia B. "They Shelve Media Openly." *Wisconsin Library Bulletin* 72 (1) (January-February 1976): 29–30.

A report covering a five-year period of a Wisconsin high school's intershelved collection concludes that "book, pamphlet and magazine losses far exceed the number of lost and damaged nonprint materials."

McNally, Paul T. *Non-book Materials in Libraries: An Annotated Bibliography.* Toowoomba, Queensland: Darling Downs Institute Press, 1979.

Sound recordings, videorecordings, transparencies, slides, filmstrips, microforms, motion pictures, pictures, maps, and games are included in this annotated bibliography arranged by broad subject category with author and title index.

McWilliams, Jerry. *The Preservation and Restoration of Sound Recordings*. Nashville, TN: American Association for State and Local History, 1979.

A thorough description of the care, handling, storage, and restoration of sound discs, tapes, cylinders, wires, and digital recordings with an emphasis on archival collections and an annotated bibliography.

The Management of Non-Book Resources in Schools. Auckland, New Zealand: Arney Road Teachers' Centre, 1981.

Pages 36–41 give brief suggestions for the processing and storage of the major types of materials.

Mann, Thomas J. "A System for Processing and Shelving Works of Mixed Media Format." *Library Resources & Technical Services* 23 (2) (Spring 1979): 163–67.

Louisiana State University Library's guidelines for the segregated storage or intershelving of materials.

Mason, Robert M. "All About Diskettes." *Library Journal* 109 (5) (March 15, 1984): 558–59.

Includes a brief description of the manufacture, marketing, and handling of floppies and microfloppies and an illustration showing the relative sizes of disk contaminants.

Midgley, Thomas Keith. "21 Oddball Ideas that Work." *Audiovisual Instruction* 21 (7) (September 1976): 43, 63.

Includes suggestions for mounting and laminating using cheap materials and unusual methods.

Miller, Shirley. *The Vertical File and Its Satellites: A Handbook of Acquisition, Processing, and Organization*. 2d ed. Library Science Text Series. Littleton, CO: Libraries Unlimited, 1979.

This practical guide for circulating collections gives advice on the care and storage of pictorial materials, maps, and to a lesser extent photographs. Adhesives, lamination, enclosed and open shelf storage methods, and a detailed description of mounting techniques are included.

Morrow, Carolyn Clark. *Conservation Treatment Procedures: A Manual of Step-by-step Procedures for the Maintenance and Repair of Library Materials*. Littleton, CO: Libraries Unlimited, 1982.

Pages 65–147 show well illustrated, easy-to-follow instructions that include a list of equipment and supplies and approximate time and cost for pamphlet binding, pressboard binding, mending with Japanese paper and starch paste, polyester film encapsulation, simple portfolios, four flap portfolios, and solander boxes.

Morrow, Carolyn Clark, and Schoenly, Steven B. *A Conservation Bibliography for Librarians, Archivists, and Administrators.* Troy, NY: Whitson, 1979.

Thirteen hundred and sixty-seven entries for works published since 1966 divided into two parts: a short classified and annotated list and a comprehensive list with a subject index.

Newiss, Joan. "Diversification and Multi-media Control: The Leeds Polytechnic Beckett Park Site Library." *Audiovisual Librarian* 7 (4) (Autumn 1981): 9–14.

Provides pros and cons of intershelving and partial intershelving.

Nichols, Harold. *Map Librarianship.* London: C. Bingley, 1976.

Pages 112–33 give a detailed discussion of archival storage, both horizontal and vertical. Brief suggestions for intershelving circulating collections are included. Pages 272–77 discuss care and preservation with emphasis on archival libraries.

One-Stop Shopping: Organizing Media for Accessibility. Stout Menomonie, WI: Produced by Instructional Technology Services, University of Wisconsin for Wisconsin Association of School Librarians, 1975. 1 book, 1 filmstrip, 1 sound cassette, 1 manual.

Discusses the advantages of intershelving in a school library.

Pacey, Philip, ed. *Art Library Manual: A Guide to Resources and Practice.* London: Bowker in association with the Art Libraries Society, 1977.

A collection of essays dealing in part with the care, handling, and storage of illustrations, art originals, microforms, sound recordings, slides, videotapes, motion pictures, and photographs.

Paris, Judith, and Boss, Richard W. "The Care and Maintenance of Videodiscs and Players." *Videodisc/Videotext* 2 (1) (Winter 1982): 38–46.

Describes the place of videodiscs in libraries, optical and capacitance systems, the care of the discs, and the maintenance of the equipment.

Preservation of Photographs. Rochester, NY: Eastman Kodak, 1979.

A detailed discussion of the care, handling, and archival storage of photographs, negatives, and film.

Raikes, Deborah A. "Microform Storage in Libraries" followed by "Survey of Microform Storage Equipment & Supplies." *Library Technology Reports* 12 (3) (July-August 1979): 445–558.

An introductory article followed by a detailed description of various storage methods with a list of manufacturers and distributors.

Rehrauer, George. *The Film User's Handbook: A Basic Manual for Managing Library Film Services*. New York: Bowker, 1975.

A brief overview of the care, handling, storage, and splicing of 8mm and 16mm motion pictures with illustrations of damaged film.

Ristow, Walter W. *The Emergence of Maps in Libraries*. Hamden, CT: Linnet, 1980.

A collection of papers published between 1939 and 1979 covers many aspects of archival and specialized map libraries and includes detailed discussions of lamination and deacidification.

Sandner, Fred, et al. *A Bibliography of the Storage and Care of Non-book Materials in Libraries With Selected Annotations*. Washington, DC: ERIC, 1979.

An extensive bibliography with many annotated citations for works published between 1922 and 1979 on film media, magnetic tapes, maps, microforms, original paintings and prints, non-original prints, sound recordings, photographs, and negatives in active collections.

Schroeder, Don, and Lare, Gary. *Audiovisual Equipment and Materials: A Basic Repair and Maintenance Manual*. Metuchen, NJ: Scarecrow, 1979.

Pages 69–77 show techniques for the basic emergency repair of 16mm sound films, filmstrips, and cassette tapes and for the cleaning of sound discs described with clear instructions accompanied by illustrations.

Seminara, Eleanor, and Coty, Patricia. "Integrated Shelving at Niagara County Community College Library Learning Center." *The Bookmark* 36 (4) (Summer 1977): 94–97.

Provides a description of the development of the library and its intershelved collection.

Sisterson, Joyce; Storey, Jan; Winkworth, Ian. "Letters—Audiovisual Integration." *Audiovisual Librarian* 7 (1) (Winter 1981): 20–21.

A strong statement in support of the value of intershelving with a brief description of an integrated collection in a British polytechnic institute library.

Soulier, J. Steven. *Real Objects and Models*. The Instructional Media Library, 12. Englewood Cliffs, NJ: Educational Technology, 1981.

Pages 63–66 have a brief discussion of care and handling of realia and models.

Spaulding, Carl M. "Kicking the Silver Habit: Confessions of a Former Addict." *American Libraries* 9 (11) (December 1978): 653–69.

A comparison of the archival storage qualities of diazo, vesicular, and silver microfilm.

Steward, Milo V. *Organizing Your 2 × 2 Slides: A Storage and Retrieval System*. Technical Leaflet, 88; History News, Vol. 31, No. 3. Nashville, TN: American Association for State and Local History, 1976.

Discusses the storage of slides in sheets of semi-rigid plastic.

Stoness, B. Jeanne. "Integration of Print and Non-print Resources." *Expression* 1 (1) (Spring 1976): 34–37. Also *NYLA Bulletin* 24 (October 1976): 1–2, 10–11.

The author, who has organized both an elementary and a secondary school library, describes her positive experiences with intershelving.

Storage and Care of Kodak Color Materials. Rochester, NY: Eastman Kodak, 1982.

A fairly detailed pamphlet for the layperson about color negatives, slides, and prints.

Storage and Preservation of Microfilm. Rochester, NY: Eastman Kodak, 197–?

Describes protection measures from fire and water, humidity control, contaminants and blemishes for microfilms in medium-term or archival storage.

Swan, Alice. "Conservation of Photographic Print Collections. *Library Trends* 30 (2) (Fall 1981): 267–96.

The care and handling of salt, albumen, collodion, gelatin, and silver image prints in archival collections.

Swartzburg, Susan G. *Preserving Library Materials: A Manual*. Metuchen, NJ: Scarecrow, 1980.

A clearly written, pragmatic overview of the care, handling, and storage of sound recordings, videotapes, art originals, maps, photographs, slides, and microforms.

Swartzburg, Susan Garretson, ed. *Conservation in the Library: A Handbook of Use and Care of Traditional and Nontraditional Materials*. Westport, CT: Greenwood Press, 1983.

A collection of essays, most of which have an overview of care, handling, and storage, includes chapters on slides, photographs, microforms, motion pictures, sound recordings, and videodiscs.

Teague, S. J. *Microform Librarianship*. 2d ed. London: Butterworth, 1979.

Pages 30–31 offer a brief overview of care and storage in British libraries.

Thompson, Anthony Hugh. *Storage, Handling and Preservation of Audiovisual Materials*. AV in action, 3. The Hague: Nederlands Bibliotheek en Lektuur Centrum, 1983.

This booklet edited by the IFLA Round Table on Audiovisual Media lists in brief point form the acceptable environmental conditions, natural life expectancy, handling, and intershelving (both total and partial) of transparencies, slides, filmstrips, motion picture loops, motion pictures, sound recordings, videotapes, videodiscs, and kits. There is some reference to archival storage.

Thompson, Donald D. "Comparing Costs: An Examination of the Real and Hidden Costs of Different Methods of Storage. *ASIS Bulletin* 7 (1) (October 1980): 14–15.

Compares the costs involved in conventional library storage, collection weeding, high density storage, and microfilming.

Tiffany, Constance J. "The War between the Stacks." *American Libraries* 9 (8) (September 1978): 499.

Gives a brief but forceful argument for intershelving.

Toy Libraries: How to Start a Toy Library in Your Community. Toronto, ON: Canadian Association of Toy Libraries, 1978.

Pamphlet includes brief suggestions for care, circulation, and repair of toys and instructions for making toy bags.

Tucker, Richard N. *The Organisation and Management of Educational Technology*. New Patterns of Learning Series. London: Croom Helm, 1979.

Pages 74–88 give a general discussion about centralizing materials, including a chart of 43 media formats with brief opinions on storage.

Veaner, Allen B. "Practical Microform Materials for Libraries: Silver, Diazo, Vesicular." *Library Resources & Technical Services* 26 (3) (July/September 1982): 306–08.

Includes concise remarks in nontechnical language about permanence and durability.

Veihman, Robert A. "Some Thoughts on Intershelving." In *Planning and Operating Media Centers*. Readings from Audiovisual Instruction, 2. Washington, DC: Association for Educational Communications and Technology, 1975.

An article that refutes anti-intershelving arguments is followed by a brief description by Robert Koelling of intershelving in some Wisconsin public school libraries.

Weihs, Jean, with Lewis, Shirley, and Macdonald, Janet. *Nonbook Materials: The Organization of Integrated Collections*. 2d ed. Ottawa, ON: Canadian Library Association, 1979.

Pages 115–19 give a concise, general description of the care and handling of film media, magnetic tapes, microscope slides, sound discs, three-dimensional materials, and two-dimensional opaque materials, with suggestions for intershelving and partial intershelving.

Weinstein, Robert A., and Booth, Larry. *Collection, Use, and Care of Historical Photographs*. Nashville, TN: American Association for State and Local History, 1978.

Pages 123–51 discuss care and handling in archival collections of photographs and negatives. Mounting techniques and a detailed appraisal of envelopes are included.

Wellisch, Hans, ed. *Nonbook Materials: A Bibliography of Recent Publications*. Student Contribution Series, No. 6. College Park, MD: University of Maryland College of Library and Information Services, 1975.

Under the subheading "Storage and Preservation" the chapters on sound recordings, maps, motion pictures, pictures, realia, slides, transparencies, filmstrips, and general works have well-annotated citations.

Weston, Murray. "The Storage and Handling of Videocassettes in Libraries." *Audiovisual Librarian* 8 (1) (Winter 1982): 31–33.

Offers very practical rules for care and handling, some comments on circulation, and a brief reference to storage.

Williams, John C. "A Review of Paper Quality and Paper Chemistry." *Library Trends* 30 (2) (Fall 1981): 203–24.

A semi-technical article and three-page bibliography about paper quality from early times to the present day, acid-free paper, deacidification, and predicting the life of paper.

Wilson, De Etta. "On the Way to Intershelving: Elements in the Decision." *Hawaii Library Association Journal* 33 (1976): 43–51.

A Hawaiian community college introduces intershelving for most of its collection.

Index

Compiled by Linda Webster

Magazines. *See* Periodicals.
Magnetic tapes. *See also* Computer tapes; Sound tapes; Videotapes.
  care and handling, 31–32, 79, 82, 84, 91, 94
  storage, 32–33, 82, 84, 91, 94
Manila envelopes. *See* Envelopes.
Manuals, 18, 19, 20, 28 (Fig. 4d), 33, 41, 42, 45, 46, 68 (Fig. 28a)
Manuscripts, 81–82
Maps
  archival preservation, 57, 78, 81–82, 87, 90, 91
  boxes and pamphlet boxes, 58, 68 (Fig. 28h)
  care and handling, 81, 82, 84, 87–88, 89, 90, 91, 92, 94
  clip-on holders, 17
  folding, 56 (Fig. 20), 56–57
  hanging devices, 20
  storage, 58, 81, 82, 84, 87–88, 89, 91, 92, 94
Media. *See* Nonbook materials.
Media centers. *See* School libraries.
Media shelves
  filmstrips, 45
  general considerations, 20
  microcomputer cassettes, 37–38
  microcomputer disks, 75
  microfilms, 51
  motion pictures, 27 (Fig. 3f), 28 (Fig. 5f), 38 (Figs. 13a, 13d), 52, 53
  slides, 38 (Fig. 13h), 47
  sound cassettes, 37–38, 38 (Fig. 13g)
  sound discs, 27–28 (Figs. 3e, 4h, 5g)
  sound tapes, 37–38, 38 (Fig. 13c)
  three-dimensional and boxed materials, 28 (Fig. 5i), 38 (Figs. 13e, 13f), 68 (Fig. 28)
  transparencies, 27 (Fig. 3g), 54
  two-dimensional opaque materials, 27 (Fig. 3h), 59–60, 60 (Fig. 22g)
Microcomputer cassettes, 17, 18, 28 (Fig. 5c), 33–38, 34 (Fig. 8), 35 (Fig. 10), 68 (Fig. 28b)
Microcomputer disks, 17, 44 (Fig. 16f), 50 (Fig. 19), 68 (Fig. 28d), 74–75, 89
Microfiches
  binders, 13 (Fig. 1b), 27 (Fig. 3c), 49 (Fig. 18), 68 (Fig. 28f)
  book-like albums, 49–50, 50 (Fig. 19)
  boxes and pamphlet boxes, 48, 60 (Fig. 22c)
  care and handling, 47, 79

Microfilms
  boxes and pamphlet boxes, 13 (Figs. 1k, 1l), 48
  care and handling, 47, 78, 79, 92
  clip-on holders, 18, 44 (Fig. 16c), 48
  media shelves, 51
  modular units, 18, 27 (Fig. 3b), 48
  storage, 78, 79, 92
Microforms
  archival preservation, 78, 92
  care and handling, 47–48, 78, 79, 80–81, 82, 83, 85, 88, 90, 91, 92, 93
  equipment, 41
  storage, 50, 78, 79, 80–81, 82, 83, 85, 88, 90–91, 92, 93
Microopaques, 13 (Fig. 1l), 48–50, 79
Microscope slides, 94
Mobile storage. *See* Cartmobiles.
Mock-ups. *See* Models.
Models, 38 (Fig. 13e), 68 (Fig. 28e), 91. *See also* Three-dimensional and boxed materials.
Modular units
  general considerations, 18
  microcomputer cassettes, 18, 36–37
  microfilms, 18, 27, (Fig. 3b), 48
  motion picture loop cartridges, 27 (Fig. 3b), 44 (Fig. 16b), 52
  sound cassettes, 18, 36 (Fig. 12), 36–37
  three-dimensional and boxed materials, 67 (Fig. 27), 67–68
Motion picture cassettes, 51
Motion picture loop cartridges
  boxes and pamphlet boxes, 13 (Fig. 1h), 52
  care and handling, 82, 93
  clip-on holders, 18, 28 (Fig. 5e), 52
  hanging devices, 53
  losses, xiv
  media shelves, 38 (Fig. 13a), 53
  modular units, 27 (Fig. 3b), 44 (Fig. 16b), 52
  storage, 51
Motion pictures
  care and handling, 11–12, 40, 51, 78, 82, 84, 86, 87, 88, 90, 91, 92, 93, 94
  cartmobiles, 30 (Fig. 7), 53
  clip-on holders, 13 (Fig. 1g), 52
  hanging devices, 53
  media shelves, 27 (Fig. 3f), 28 (Fig. 5f), 52
  racks, 28 (Fig. 5f), 52
  storage, 51, 78, 82, 84, 86, 87, 88, 90, 91, 92, 93, 94